M000266744

Freedmen of the Frontier

Volume 2
Selected Creek and Seminole
Freedmen Families

Freedmen of the Frontier

Volume 2

Selected Creek and Seminole
Freedmen Families

by Angela Y. Walton-Raji

Palmyra, VA
Shortwood Press
2020

© 2020 Angela Y. Walton-Raji
All rights reserved.

Front cover: "Map of Indian Territory," from
*Johnson Directory and Atlas Company. Business atlas ;
every office favorite.* Chicago : Johnson Directory and Atlas Co., 1888.
Courtesy of the Oklahoma Historical Society.

Edited and formatted by Jean L. Cooper.

ISBN-13: 978-0-9998182-0-6 (v. 1)
ISBN-10: 0-9998182-0-1 (v. 1)
ISBN-13: 978-0-9998182-1-3 (v. 2)
ISBN-10: 0-9998182-1-X (v. 2)

No part of this publication may be reproduced or transmitted in any form or by any means, electronic or mechanical, including photocopy, recording, or any information storage and retrieval system now known or to be invented, without permission in writing from the publisher and author, except by a reviewer who wishes to quote brief passages in connection with a review written for inclusion in a magazine, newspaper, or broadcast.

Dedication

This two-volume set is dedicated to the Freedmen of the Five Tribes,
who were once enslaved in Indian Territory.

May their legacy be forever honored,
and may their presence on the soil of
what is now Oklahoma never be forgotten.

Table of Contents

Acknowledgments

Since Volume 1 was published in 2019, the response from the community of Oklahoma Freedmen descendants has been amazing. Several readers have even found their own families reflected on the pages of the book, while others were simply overjoyed to see a work reflecting their ancestral community. This second volume completes the documentation of the 52 families profiled in the original 52-week project that began in 2017.

Much appreciation is owed to many who have been supporters of this initiative. From east to west coast and more importantly, from Oklahoma, the response has been extremely supportive. In this second volume appreciation must be shown to those who graciously shared images of their ancestors. Special thanks to Lesa Myers Engram, for permission to use her ancestor Hagar Myers' photo in the chapter describing her ancestor's contribution to bringing an end to the Green Peach War. Likewise, special thanks is also given to Susie Moore who several years ago generously shared an image of Caesar Bruner, founder and leader of the Bruner band in the Seminole Nation. Her image is one of the very few images of Seminole leaders we have from the nineteenth century. Also a special thanks to Charles Gibson who generously shared an obituary of Benjamin Bruner and a photograph of the headstone of Caesar Bruner.

Thank you to the Oklahoma Historical Society (OHS) for permission to use their resources, including the cover map on these two volumes. In addition, the partnership of the Oklahoma Historical Society with Ancestry.com made other images now accessible quickly, which has expanded opportunities for research through records that predate the Dawes era.

Finally, I appreciate Freedmen descendants for their many contributions over the years to the African-Native American message board on the AfriGeneas website. Their energy is still visible now on social media and continues through their contributions and continued dialogue. The devotion of these descendants to continued research of their history has clearly filled a void in Oklahoma/Indian Territory history.

I am particularly grateful for the works of scholars Daniel F. Littlefield, Kevin Mulroy, and Claudio Saunt, whose research about African-ancestored Creeks and Seminoles have become critical resources for students of Creek and Seminole Freedmen history. I hope many will be inspired to find their own family histories because of their scholarly works.

The efforts of the Creek Freedmen's descendants should be noted, as their struggles for inclusion in the Muscogee nation are currently playing out in the legal system. Descendants' groups have emerged in Oklahoma in recent years, and the actions of the Muscogee Creek Freedmen Band continue to highlight the amazingly rich history of Creek Freedmen and their legacy. Likewise, the two Freedmen bands in the Seminole Nation continue to seek full citizen status with the benefits that come with citizenship. May the Dosar Barkus and Caesar Bruner bands continue to thrive and remain in their nation as full citizens.

This second volume seeks to honor some of the ancestors from both nations.

Angela Y. Walton-Raji
June 19, 2020

Sources

The documents used in this work come from a set of records in the National Archives and Records Administration. The original records are kept at the Federal Records Center in Fort Worth, Texas. The records are part of the larger holdings of the Records of the Bureau of Indian Affairs, 1868-1914, Record Group 75, NAI Number: 251747.

In the 1970s, the original records were microfilmed and separate microfilm publications were made by the National Archives. These are now cataloged under those publication numbers for researchers. At the beginning of each chapter in this work, images of the enrollment cards (also known as census cards) are shown. Note that in many cases with Creek Freedmen, the "Field" number is sometimes cited alongside the Enrollment Card number, and that will occasionally be reflected with some files.

Enrollment Cards

The microfilmed images of enrollment cards are cataloged as National Archives Microfilm Publication Number M1186. There are 93 rolls in this collection. In recent years, Ancestry.com and Fold3.com have digitized the enrollment cards and made them available online. The images found on Ancestry.com were scanned and digitized in color from the original cards. Fold3.com has digitized black-and-white images of the microfilmed collection.

On Ancestry.com, the enrollment cards are titled: *Oklahoma and Indian Territory, Dawes Census Cards for Five Civilized Tribes, 1898-1914* [database on-line]. Provo UT, USA: Ancestry.com Operations, Inc. 2014.

On Fold3.com, the enrollment cards are titled: *Dawes Enrollment Cards*, Source: National Archives, Publication Number M1186, Published June 4, 2009.

Application Jackets

The application jackets that contain interviews, affidavits, letters, and other records are cataloged as National Archives Microfilm Publication Number M1301. There are 438 rolls of microfilm in this collection. The application jackets have also been digitized and placed online through Ancestry.com and Fold3.com. Both services provide identical records.

On Ancestry.com the application jackets are titled: *U.S., Native American Applications for Enrollment in the Five Civilized Tribes, 1898-1914* [database on-line]. Provo, UT, USA: Ancestry.com Operations Inc., 2013.

On Fold3.com, these records are titled: *Dawes Packets*, Source, National Archives, Publication Number M1301, Published March 7, 2008.

Land Allotment Records

The records pertaining to the land allotments are part of a collection at the National Archives titled: Department of the Interior. Office of Indian Affairs. Five Civilized Tribes Agency. *Applications for Allotment compiled 1899-1907. Textual records.* Records of the Bureau of Indian Affairs, Record Group 75. These records are found on both Ancestry.com and FamilySearch.org.

On Family Search, the collection citation is: *Oklahoma Applications for Allotment, Five Civilized Tribes, 1899-1907.* Database with images. Family Search.org: 17 October 2016, National Archives and Records Administration, Southwest Region, Fort Worth, Texas.

The same collection is on Ancestry.com, and cataloged as: *Oklahoma and Indian Territory, Land Allotment Jackets for Five Civilized Tribes, 1884-1934* [database on-line]. Provo, UT, USA: Ancestry.com Operations, Inc., 2014.

U.S. Federal Census, Slave Schedule of 1860

The U.S. Census Slave Schedules are also used in this document. The source of the slave schedule of 1860 is: United States of America, Bureau of the Census. *Eighth Census of the United States, 1860.* Washington, D.C.: National Archives and Records Administration, 1860. M653, 1,438 rolls. Note that the slave schedule in Indian Territory is actually part of the microfilm rolls for Arkansas. At the National Archives the separate reel of microfilm pertaining to Indian Territory is called *Lands West of Arkansas.*

On Ancestry.com, the slave schedules for Indian Territory appear under the listing for the state of Arkansas as "Cherokee Nation," "Choctaw Nation," "Chickasaw Nation," etc. All are documented as "counties." The slave schedules will appear in the drop-down menu in alphabetical order.

The 1860 slave census is also available on the free online site The Internet Archive (www.archive.org). The Internet Archive also provides free access to the Indian Census of the United States from 1885 to 1940 at (https://archive.org/details/indian_census). The microfilms that were scanned to provide these images were provided to the Internet Archive courtesy of the Allen County Public Library, in Fort Wayne, Indiana.

Part 1. Creek Freedmen

Creek Freedmen—An Introduction

Africans in Indian Territory have an amazingly rich history. Having arrived in the 1840s and '50s, their story took an unusual turn during the Civil War, when many Creeks fled into Kansas to avoid the turmoil of the War. Under the leadership of Chief Opothole Yahola, many of the enslaved Creeks arrived in the free state of Kansas having endured a very difficult journey northward. Upon entering Kansas, enslaved Creeks and some Cherokees now found themselves upon free soil, and many accepted the challenges of joining the conflict by enlisting in the Union Army. The soldiers of the 1st and 2nd Kansas Colored Infantries were among the first men of African descent to enter the conflict of the Civil War and were the first to see battle in the conflict at Island Mound, Missouri, in 1862. Later in the war, these units were re-designated as the 79th and 83rd U.S. Colored Troops. Meanwhile, other African Creeks found themselves also in the military, choosing to enlist in the 1st, 2nd, and 3rd Indian Home Guards. Those who were bilingual and spoke the Muscogee language were especially useful serving in the Home Guards.

After the Civil War, Creek Freedmen emerged as essential contributors to society, many serving as interpreters for the tribe. More than once delegations were sent to Washington, DC to negotiate on behalf of the tribe, and Creek Freedmen were in those delegations. In addition, some leaders such as Harry Island, Ketch Barnett, Cow Tom also worked on behalf of the Freedmen and sought to insure that they would be treated as full citizens within their nation. As the structure of the Muscogee Nation stabilized after the war and the nation carved out the tribal town system, three Freedmen tribal towns, named Arkansas, Canadian, and North Fork, emerged as well. The towns to which the Freedmen belonged were duly noted on each Dawes enrollee's cards in the years before statehood.

The structure of the tribal town system also ensured that Freedmen would be a part of the governing structure of the tribe. Creek Freedmen served in both ruling houses—the House of Warriors and the House of Kings. Each tribal town had a representative in the House of Warriors and each town had a "Town King" serving in the House of Kings. In that history the stories of men such as Sugar T. George can be found. He had a rich history serving in both ruling houses and participated in multiple affairs of the Nation. Sugar George also served as a soldier in the Indian Home Guards, and later had roles as an attorney and tribal leader.

The efforts of Creek Freedmen to seek education was reflected in the schools that emerged. When the Creek Indians abandoned Tullahassee Mission, Creek Freedmen put their energy into making Tullahassee Manual Labor School a viable place for the education of their own children. The Creek Seminole College in Boley, Oklahoma, was another establishment that Freedmen from both tribes used. And in the city of Muskogee, Evangel Mission was a Baptist-sponsored primary school option for Creek Freedmen and Indian children.

It should be noted that many resources were used to find data on these families. In some cases a name was spelled one way on the Dawes cards, and years later during the Pioneer Interviews from the 1930s, the spelling was different. This is noted in the cases of the surname Fulsom, sometimes written as Folsom. This was also the case where the name Myers was written years later as Meyers. Extensive research was done to insure that there were not two distinct people, with similar names, and that in both cases they were the same person.

From the Dunn Roll, through the years of per capita payments to the Dawes era, the bilingual and bi-cultural Freedmen were an integral part of their nation. Some of the rich histories of Freedmen families are reflected here.

The Family of Elijah Canard

Many who research the Freedmen from the Muscogee Creek Nation are aware that there are challenges facing the researcher, because many of the application jackets containing interviews were never microfilmed, thus never digitized, and now are lost. Although a good portion of Creek records are missing, there are some cases in which interviews survived, and they are worth examining. Using sources beyond the Dawes Rolls, and examining some of those university-held records and interviews of former slaves, we can still find multiple stories about Freedmen families of the Muscogee Creek Nation. The family of Elijah Canard is such a family whose history can be examined and studied at length.

Front of Creek Enrollment Card #221

In August 1898, Elijah Canard appeared in front of the Dawes Commission to enroll himself and his family as Creek Freedmen. Though Creeks, they resided in the Chickasaw Nation, in the town of Maxwell, Indian Territory. James Canard and the children had been recognized as Creeks prior to that, and their names were already on a Creek roll in 1895. At this time, Elijah was enrolling his sons, James, Jimmie, and Johnie in addition to two great-nephews, Earnest and Wilford McIntosh.

The family information found on many enrollment cards illustrates how many Creek families were blended with families from other nations. In this particular case the Creek Canard family is blended with a family of Chickasaw Freedmen, and the information is captured on the notes found on the bottom of the same card. The notes are full of information—clues to more data—and they can all lead the researcher to explore additional records and find even more.

Elijah was forty-one years old at the time, and he had been enslaved by Motey Canard. Prior to Elijah's appearance before the Dawes Commission, his name had been inscribed on the 1867 Dunn Roll, and this was noted on the enrollment card as well. (On the 1867 Dunn Roll, Elijah's name appeared as Elijah McIntosh, #934.) Elijah's name was also written on the 1890 Roll of Creek citizens as having belonged to Arkansas Town.

McIntoshes of Arkansas in the 1867 Dunn Roll.

Citizenship in the Creek Nation was organized by tribal towns. There were 14 tribal "towns" and three of them were "colored" tribal towns. Arkansas, North Fork, and Canadian "Colored" towns were part of the tribal town structure. Belonging to a "town" did not mean that one resided in a place that bore that name. It meant that they were affiliated with the "town," and they were considered "members" of the political structure called a town, but it was not a visible place on a map. It was a structured political district. This is sometimes confusing, and in recent years there have been maps created locating these "towns" as North Fork Colored, Arkansas Colored, and Canadian Colored. However, the reality is that many who "belonged" to a town often resided in communities such as Muskogee, Okmulgee, Coweta, and other places. The closest comparison might be the modern day concept of "precincts" which are not physical places on a map, yet they are districts to which citizens belong and vote, and elected representatives carry on other duties for that district.

Elijah's father was Caesar Canard, who was enslaved by Motey Canard. Elijah's mother was Clara Hared, enslaved by Maria McIntosh. Both parents apparently died immediately after the Civil War. By the time of the Dawes Commission, Elijah Canard belonged to North Fork Town. James's mother was Tilda

Canard. The mother of Jimmie and Johnie was listed as Leathy Canard. Elijah's wife in 1898 was said to be Martha Canard, a Chickasaw Freedman.[1]

Back of Creek Enrollment Card #221

Anthony and Peggy McIntosh were the parents of Elijah's great-nephews whose names appeared on the front of the card. Their father Anthony was not a citizen, but their mother Peggy was a Creek Freedman who belonged to North Fork Town. Peggy was the niece of Elijah and the mother of Earnest and Wilford McIntosh, the two young boys. All had their citizenship approved by the Creek Council in August 1895.

From the Application Jacket:

We are thankful that a detailed interview reflecting this Creek Freedman family is included in the file. However, the file actually reflects an enrollment case of Earnest and Wilford McIntosh, not Elijah Canard. This interview still reveals much detail about the two young children in the Canard household.

The first person interviewed was Polly Perry. She was a sister of Elijah, but she was there to testify on behalf of the two boys, Ernest and Wilford McIntosh. The mother of the two boys, Peggy McIntosh, was deceased at the time of the interview. Both Polly and Peggy's mother were siblings of Elijah Canard. Polly explained the relationship in her interview.

DEPARTMENT OF THE INTERIOR
COMMISSION TO THE FIVE CIVILIZED TRIBES
MUSKOGEE LAND OFFICE, JULY 11, 1900

In the matter of the application of Earnest McIntosh and Wilford McIntosh for enrollment as citizens of the Creek Nation.

Polly Perry, being duly sworn by G.L.V. Emerson, a notary public testified as follows.
(By Mr. Angel)

Q. Is your name Polly Perry? A. Yes, sir.
Q. How old are you? A. I couldn't tell my age, exactly how old I am

---

[1] I should point out that tribal towns were often places of belonging, and did not reflect actual residence.

Q. About how old are you? A. We never had our number put down; I couldn't tell how old I am.

Q. Do you think you are about 54? A. I might be that, I guess.

Q. Are you a citizen of the Creek nation? A. Yes, sir.

Q. What Creek town do you belong to? A. Northfork.

Q. What is your post office address? A. Bearden, Creek Nation.

Q. How long have you resided at Bearden? A. It has been 9 or ten years since I have been living there.

Q. Do you know applicants for citizenship, Earnest and Wilford McIntosh? A. My brother raised the children, and he would know better than I do; about 8 or 9 he says.

Q. Do you think Earnest is 8 or 9 years old? A. Yes, sir.

Q. Wilford is younger? A. Yes, sir. He was the baby when his mother died.

Q. What kin are those children to you? A. Their mother was my niece. She was my sister's daughter, and her mother is dead. So is Wilford's mother; they are orphan children and have no mother.

Q. What is the name of the mother of these children? A. Peggy McIntosh.

Q. What kin was Peggy McIntosh to you? A. She was my niece

Q. Do you now about how old Peggy McIntosh was when she died? A. No, sir, I don't exactly know how old she was when she died; never had her age down at all.

Q. Would she have been as old as Elijah Canard? A. She was younger than Elijah when she died.

Q. Do you know about how long ago she died? A. It has been about four years since she died.

Q. Where did Peggy live during her life time? A. In the Chickasaw.

Q. Who was the father of these children? A. The father of them is a state man. His name is Anthony McIntosh.

Q. Is he living? A. Yes, sir, he is living

Q. Do those children live with him? A. My brother raised the children after the mother died.

Q. Is Lige Canard your full brother? A. Yes sir, one mother and one father.

On the second page of the interview Elijah himself speaks and shares more information about the family, including details about the father of the two boys.

Q. Is this Canard sitting in the chair? A. Yes sir, that is him.

Q. Is Miley Johnson a full sister of yours? A. Yes sir, full sister of mine. One father, and one mother.

Q. Is this Miley Johnson? A. Yes sir, that is her; she is my sister.

Q. Have you any other brothers and sisters? A. Yes sir, there is 4 of us; full brothers and sisters.

Q. Nelson Canard is the older brother? A. Yes sir, the oldest of us all.

Q. Did you attend the wedding of Nelson and Phoebe McIntosh? A. No, sir, I didn't.

Q. How do you know they are married then? A. The minister went to marry them, and they were married at my brother Nelson Canard's house.

Q. Why didn't you go? A. We didn't go to the wedding.

Q. You can state here under oath that Nathan McIntosh and Peggy McIntosh were legally married by a minister. A. Yes, sir, by a minister, and they lived together as man and wife.

Q. Up to the time of her death excepting during the time he was in the penitentiary? A. Yes, sir.

* * *

ELIJAH CANARD, being duly sworn by G. L. V. Emerson, a Notary Public, testified as follows:

(By Mr. Angel)

Q. What town do you belong to? A. Northfork.

Q. Are you a citizen of the Creek Nation? A. Yes sir.

Q. What is your post office address? A. Maxwell, I. T.

Q. How old are you? A. I expect that I am 35 or 40 years old.

Q. Do you know the applicants for citizenship; Earnest and Wilford McIntosh? A. Yes, sir.

Q. How long have you known them? A. All their lives. They were born and raised right with me.

Q. Who was the father of those children? A. The mother said Nathan McIntosh was the father of them.

Q. Is he a citizen of any nation? A. He was a United States citizen.

Q. Is he now living? A. Yes, sir.

Q. Where does he reside? A. He lives in the Chickasaw Nation.

Q. Are these children living with him? A. No sir, they are living with me.

Q. Was Nathan McIntosh married to Peggy McIntosh? A. Yes, sir.

Q. Were you present at the wedding? A. No sir, I wasn't at the wedding.

Q. How do you know they were married? A. I saw people who were at the wedding and they were married in the neighborhood where I live, and I suppose they were from what people said.

Q. Were they married by a minister, according to the laws of the Chickasaw nation? A. Yes, sir, I suppose so.

Q. I want to know what you know. A. Yes sir, of course they were not getting out licenses like they are now.

Q. Were they married by a minister? A. Yes, sir.

Q. How long did they live together as man and wife? A. 12 or 13 years, probably.

Q. Did they live together up to the time of the death of Peggy? A. No sir, when she died he was off to the penitentiary.

Q. Did you ever have the names of those children placed on either the Choctaw or Chickasaw rolls? A. No sir, I never have.

Q. Do you know whether or not their names have ever been placed upon the Choctaw or Chickasaw Nation? A. No sir, their names have never been placed on the Choctaw or Chickasaw.

Q. They never drew any money in the Choctaw or Chickasaw Nation? A. No sir, never drew any money.

Q. What kin are you to these children? A. I don't know what you would call it. I was the uncle of these children's mother; I consider I am the children's uncle.

Q. The grandmother of these children was your sister? A. Yes, sir, she was my sister.

Q. Was she a Creek citizen? A. Yes, sir, she was owned by the Creeks.

Q. She was owned by a Creek Citizen? A. My sister, Wat Grayson owned them both.

Q. Do you know how old Peggie [sic] was when she died? A. No sir, I don't know, 34 or 35, maybe a little older than that. She was 30 odd years old.

Q. That was 4 or 5 years ago. A. She's been dead 4 years ago; close to 40 [sic] I expect.

Q. Do you know whether Peggy's name was ever put on the Dunn Roll or not? A. I suppose so, I couldn't say whether it was or not.

Q. Was she here at the time? A. Yes, she was here at the time.

Q. In the Creek Nation? A. Yes, sir.

Q. When did she go to the Choctaw Nation? A. I couldn't tell you exactly when she went to the Chickasaw Nation; it was some 4 or 5 years; after the surrender she went; I couldn't tell.

Q. About how old is Earnest McIntosh? A. Earnest is 9 years old. Will be 10 this coming November.

Q. How old is Wilford? A. He is going on six.

Q. They are now both alive? A. Yes sir, they were when I left home Sunday.

Q. Have they any brothers and sisters? A. They have a brother, but no sister.

Q. A full brother? A. No sir, half- brother.

Q. What was his name? A. Andrew Johnson.

Q. Do you know whether these children participated in the 1895 payment in the Creek Nation? A. Yes, sir, both of them drawed then.

Q. Did Earnest draw in the 1890 payment? A. Yes, sir.

Q. How do you know that? A. I was there are the time of the payment, and if the payment was that year, he drawed.

Q. How much money did he draw that year? A. I think, $29.

Q. Did you draw the money for him? A. The mother drawed it.

Q. His mother? A. Yes, sir.

Q. Did you know George McIntosh? A. I don't believe I do.

Q. Did you know Andrew McIntosh? A. No sir; oh yes, she is dead now and that Andrew McIntosh is the Andrew Johnson I was telling you about.

Q. Who was the owner of Peggy McIntosh? A. She must have been a slave under Wat Grayson; her mother was and she was born there.

Q. Who was your owner? A. My owner was Mariah Perry and Hardridge; I know the last husband she lived with was McIntosh

Q. How did you get the name of Elijah Canard? A. I got that by my mother belonging to Motey Canard. I suppose there is where I got the Canard name.

Q. It says on your card that you were a slave of Motey Canard. How does that happen? A. I couldn't tell that.

Q. Didn't you come before the Dawes Commission to be enrolled? A. No, sir.

Q. Who did? A. My brother Nelson Canard.

Q. It isn't correct then that you were a slave of Motey Canard. A. I suppose it is not if it is that way, no sir.

Q. Nelson Canard is your brother? A. Yes sir.

Q. And Miley Johnson and Polly Perry are your sisters? A. Yes, sir.

Q. It is Polly Perry that has just testified is it? A. Yes, sir.

Q. Did you ever apply in the Choctaw or Chickasaw Nation for the enrollment of these children? A. No sir, I never have.

Q. Your wife is a Chickasaw? A. Yes, sir.

Q. Do you know whether anyone ever applied to the Dawes Commission for the enrollment of these children in any other nation except the Creek? A. No sir, there was nobody ever made any application for enrollment outside the Creek Nation.

Q. You made application for their enrollment as Creek citizens on the ground that their parents were owned by Creek Indians. A. Yes, sir.

Q. Have these children always lived in Indian Territory? A. Yes, sir.

Q. Have they been outside of it? A. No sir, never have.

Q. You have taken and had charge of these children for the last few years. A. Yes sir, I have had them you might say, all their lives. Their mother lived with me. Her and her husband lived with me until shortly before she died, and went to Winnewood [*sic*] and lived there a year or more and died. I took them back and have had them ever since. They ain't been away from me over 8 or 10 months of their lives.

More is revealed in the application jacket of Elijah, where there is much interest in the enrollment of the nephews, their parents, and whether they had been previously enrolled by the Creek Nation. Details about their movement during and after the Civil War, is revealed when Miley Johnson was interviewed. She explains where they were taken during the war and where the family, including Elijah lived after the war ended. And yet again, there was still interest in the status of the children and the need to determine if they had even been enrolled as Chickasaw Freedmen, as their mother was from Chickasaw Freedmen communities.

A year later, in September 1901, and then again in October, the status of Elijah (Lige) Canard was examined more thoroughly by the Commission.

DEPARTMENT OF THE INTERIOR
COMMISSION TO THE FIVE CIVILIZED TRIBES
Muskogee, Indian Territory, September 28, 1901

In the matter of the application of Elijah Canard to elect to have minor children Jimmie and Johnnie Canard enrolled as citizens of the Creek Nation, Elijah Canard being sworn testified as follows:

By the Commission:

Q. What is your name? A. Elijah Canard
Q. What is your age? About 35
Q. What is your post office address? A. Maxwell.
Q. Have you been listed for enrollment as a citizen of the Creek Freedman? A. Yes, sir.
The records of the Commission show that Elijah Canard is listed for enrollment on Creek Freedman card, field number 228.
Q. Have Jimmie and Johnnie, your minor children been listed for enrollment as citizens of the Creek Nation? A. Yes, sir.

The records of the Commission show that Jimmie and Johnnie Canard are listed for enrollment on Creek Freedmen card Field number 228.

Q. Have these children also been recognized as citizens of the Chickasaw Nation? A. No sir. They never have.
Q. If it should be found that these children have been recognized as citizens of

both the Chickasaw and Creek Nations, as citizens of what nation do you now elect to have them enrolled and receive allotments of land and share in the distribution of moneys? A. Creek Nation.

R. B. Eisenberg, being duly sworn states, as stenographer to the Commission to the Five Civilized Tribes that the above, and foregoing is a true and correct transcript of his stenographic notes of the testimony taken in the above mentioned cause.

R. B. Eisenberg

Subscribed and sworn to me before me at Muskogee, Indian Territory, this 7th day of October, 1901.

Tams Bixby,
Acting Chairman

Also in the file were two pages pertaining to the lands allotted to some of the members of the family, including the sons Jimmie and Johnnie. In the documents, the Commission noted that their mother was Chickasaw, and that they were applying as Creek Freedmen. Elijah's name was analyzed, to determine whether it was Canard, or Walker. The name Walker does not appear on the enrollment card, but comes out in this application jacket.

Willie Cohee of the Chickasaw Nation had previously made application for the boys to be enrolled as Chickasaw Freedmen and that lands were to have been allotted to them as such. The exact description of the land appears in those pages shown above.

Further analysis concluded that there were no conflicting interests in spite of the lands set aside for the sons, and that no attempt to convey the lands to them occurred, so it was decided that the Chickasaw allotments be stricken and that the Canards be enrolled and receive their Creek allotments.

Since there was much discussion about the lands allotted to the children, I decided to see where their allotted lands were located. It appears that they received land near each other, in Township 19, Range 8. The lands reflecting their family allotments are shown in the letter and map on the following pages.[2]

We do not know whether the family retained the land over the years. Many Creeks lost land due to land thieves and swindlers, who took advantage of many families in rural communities throughout Oklahoma. Hopefully this family was able to retain lands over the next century. Regardless, theirs is a history of survival of slavery, freedom, Creek citizenship, membership in their tribal town, and finally ownership of their own land after the Dawes Rolls were finally closed.

---

[2] Ancestry.com. *Oklahoma and Indian Territory, Land Allotment Jackets for Five Civilized Tribes, 1884-1934* [database on-line]. Provo, UT, USA: Ancestry.com Operations, Inc, 2014. (Creek Freedmen: Image 42 of 869).

Copy.   1-1744

L-F-T
123494-14
J. D. C.

Duplicate enrollment   March 27, 1915.
and allotment of Jimmie
and Johnie Canard or
Walker.

The Honorable

         The Secretary of the Interior.

Sir:

         I have the honor to transmit herewith the papers
in the matter of the duplicate enrollment and allotment of
Jimmie and Johnie Canard or Walker.

         The names of Jimmie and Johnie Calard appear on
the Creek freedmen roll, opposite Nos. 788 and 789, respectively, and the names of Jimmie and Johnie Walker appear
on the Chickasaw freedmen roll, opposite Nos. 1444 and 1445.

         A hearing held on April 19, 1910, to determine
whether the Creek allottees, Jimmie and Johnie Canard were
identical with the Chickasaw allottees, Jimmie and Johnie
Walker establishes such to be the fact.

         The father of the freedmen allottees in question
was Elijah Canard or Walker, and their mother was Lethia
Cohee.   The father, Elijah, was during the period of
slavery owned by a family by the name of Canard, and it
appears it was the custom for the slaves to be called by
the name of their masters. His real name appears to
have been that of Walker. Elijah Canard or Walker made

**Page 1 of a Letter re: Duplicate enrollment and allotment of
Jimmie and Johnie Canard or Walker, dated March 27, 1915.**[3]

---

[3] Chickasaw Freedman Packet #228 , in "Applications for Enrollment of the Commission to the Five Civilized Tribes, 1898-
1914," National Archives Publication M1301. https://www.fold3.com/image/260/66326255

applications for enrollment on behalf of himself and his sons,
Jimmie and Johnie as freedmen members of the Creek Nation,
and they were duly enrolled as such. A short time thereafter
Willie Cohee, who had married the mother of Jimmie and Johnie
Canard subsequent to her separation from Elijah, made application for enrollment as a Chickasaw freedmen on behalf of
himself and others, including his stepchildren, Jimmie and
Johnie Walker, and they were regularly enrolled and allotted
lands in the Chickasaw Nation. The lands allotted to Jimmie
and Johnie Walker as Chickasaw freedmen, Roll Nos. 1444 and
1445, respectively, are as follows:

> Jimmie Walker: N/2 of the SE/4 of the NE/4
> of Section 23, Township 5 North, Range 1 East;
> S/2 of the NW/4 of the SE/4 and the SW/4 of the
> NE/4 of the SE/4 of Section 12, Township 1 South,
> Range 1 West.

> Johnie Walker: S/2 of the SE/4 of the NE/4
> of Section 23, Township 5 North, Range 1 East;
> N/2 of the SW/4 of the SE/4 and the NW/4 of the
> SE/4 of the SE/4 of Section 12, Township 1 South
> Range 1 West.

On November 13, 1914, the then supervisor in charge
of the office of the superintendent for the Five Civilized
Tribes recommended that opposite the names of the above-
mentioned allottees in the Chickasaw Nation, the following
notation be made:

> Not entitled to an allotment as a Chickasaw
> freedman. Enrolled and allotted in the Creek Nation.

It was also set forth in the letter of the supervisor in charge that reconveyance deeds have been made a
matter of record, and lands described in the Chickasaw al-

**Page 2 of a Letter re: Duplicate enrollment and allotment of
Jimmie and Johnie Canard or Walker, dated March 27, 1915.**

lotments have been indicated on the allotment deeds as vacant,
and would be offered at the next sale of unallotted land
authorized by the Department.

On November 21, 1914, this Office requested that
the deeds whereby the allotments of Jimmie and Johnie Walker
as Chickasaw freedmen were reconveyed to the Choctaw and
Chickasaw Nations be forwarded to this Office. Under date
of December 29, 1914, the Acting Supervisor in Charge of
the office of the Superintendent for the Five Civilized
Tribes, submitted a copy of the reconveyance deeds, together
with a supplemental report in the matter.

The papers in this case show that the records of
conveyance of Garvin County, Oklahoma, have been examined
and it does not appear that any attempt has been made to convey the land allotted to Jimmie and Johnie Walker as Chickasaw freedmen, and consequently no conflicting interests are
involved.

There appears to have been a number of conveyances
made of the lands in the Creek Nation, but inasmuch as the
Chickasaw allotments are free from any cloud on the title
and are the lands which the allottees desire to relinquish
it is immaterial as to the status of the Creek allotments.

Deeds reconveying to the Choctaw and Chickasaw
Nations the land recently allotted have been obtained.
Said deeds are herewith and they appear all sufficient to

**Page 3 of a Letter re: Duplicate enrollment and allotment of
Jimmie and Johnie Canard or Walker, dated March 27, 1915.**

revert the title in the Choctaw and Chickasaw Nationa. It
is therefore recommended that there be placed upon the approved Chickasaw freedmen rolls in the Department, the office
of Indian Affairs and the office of the superintendent for
the Five Civilized Tribes, opposite the name of Jimmie
Walker at No. 1444 the following notation:

> Duplicate enrollment. Not entitled to an allot-
> ment as a Chickasaw freedman. Enrolled and al-
> lotted in the Creek Nation. See No. 788 Creek
> freedman roll.

and opposite the name of Johnie Walker at number 1445 the
notation:

> Duplicate enrollment. Not entitled to an allot-
> ment as a Chickasaw freedman. Enrolled and al-
> lotted in the Creek Nation. See No. 789 Creek
> freedman roll.

It is further recommended that the Superintendent
for the Five Civilized Tribes be directed to cause said deeds
of reconveyance to be properly recorded on the records of
Garvin County, Oklahoma.

> Respectfully,
>
> E. B. Merett,
> Assistant Commissioner.

3-26-WJG

Approved: Apr.5, 1915.

> Signed) Bo Sweeney,
> Assistant Secretary.

**Page 4 of a Letter re: Duplicate enrollment and allotment of
Jimmie and Johnie Canard or Walker, dated March 27, 1915.**

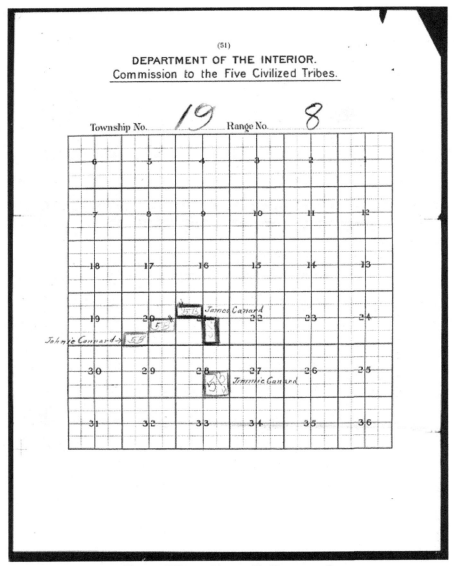

Chart of Township no.19, Range no.8.

This particular case demonstrates the complex nature of the lives of Indian Territory Freedmen. Many married citizens of other nations. Though this family lived in Chickasaw country, they were indeed Creeks and thus were entitled to lands as Creek citizens. The family's structure was complicated by the fact that Elijah Canard was the guardian to his niece's children, whose parents had preceded them in death. However, their legacy continues deeply rooted as Creeks in heritage and history.

The Family and Legacy of Lucinda Davis

Lucinda Davis.
Photograph courtesy of Oklahoma Historical Society.

Lucinda Davis's story is amazing. It was captured by both the Dawes records as well as the WPA Slave Narrative project. Lucinda was born before the Civil War, and lived well into the twentieth century. A rare photo of her was provided during the time of the WPA interviews and is shown above. During the Dawes commission era, she was married to Anderson Davis who appeared at the Dawes Commission hearings with the purpose of enrolling his family as Creek Freedmen. Her family's story is found within those records.

Anderson Davis was forty-five years of age at the time, and it appears that Anderson was not born enslaved, but was actually born a free man. However, his wife, Lucinda, was born enslaved by a Muscogee Creek Indian known as "Tuskena" or as she called him, *Tuskaya-hiniha*.

There were many children in the household, including Hayman, Serena, Adam, Josephine, Belle, Minnie, Rebecca, Lennie, and Anderson Jr. In addition to their own children, they took care of grandchildren Willie McIntosh, David Nero, and Henry Davis. The family resided near Broken Arrow and

Coweta Town, but they belonged to Arkansas Town. Their personal data was all inscribed on Creek Enrollment Card #825.

It is important to point out that there were many individuals who were placed on "Freedman" cards although they had never been "freed" from bondage, because they were born free. This was the case of Lucinda's husband, Anderson. However, as the Dawes process unfolded and the strong influence of the American policy of treating those of African ancestry differently, one will find many cases such as this where one who was born free was still classified as a "freedman."

Front of Creek Enrollment Card #825

Back of Creek Enrollment Card #825

Anderson's parents were Joseph Davidson and Becky Marshall. They were not listed on the card with a slaveholder, suggesting that they too were free born. There were many Creeks who were of African ancestry who were born free and lived as free people in the tribe, and it appears that Anderson and his family were among them.

However, Lucinda's family was different. She herself was born enslaved, and her parents were in fact enslaved by Creek Leader Opotholeyahola. From Creek Enrollment Card #825 it is also clear that the family members all belonged to Arkansas Town in the Creek Nation, and their story is one that is clearly entrenched in the tribe.

No application jacket appears for this Creek family, and one can assume that it is lost in the maze of several hundred interview packets that were never microfilmed and possibly destroyed. However, in spite of the missing interview, much rich data still remains about the Davis family. They were approved by the Dawes commission, and later applied for and receive their land allotment.

Land Allotment Jackets

Anderson Davis went through several interviews pertaining to their selection of land. Several records appear in those files reflecting the selection of land and the persons to whom the land would be allotted. The Land Allotment Jackets reveal much detail about his selection of land for himself and for others in the household. Because many of the interviews are similar and ask the same questions, I include a transcription of only one of the interviews here below.

DEPARTMENT OF THE INTERIOR
COMMISSION TO THE FIVE CIVILIZED TRIBES
MUSCOGEE, I. T., SEPT. 12TH, 1899

ANDERSON DAVIS, being sworn and examined, testified as follows:

Q. What is your name? A. Anderson Davis
Q. Are you a member of the Muscogee Nation. A. Yes, sir.
Q. What town do you belong to? A. Arkansas.
Q. Is your name on the Dunn Roll? A. Yes, sir.
Q. How did you become a citizen? A. By adoption.
Q. How long have you lived in the Creek Nation? A. Bred and born here.
Q. Have you been outside of the Indian Territory in the last two years? A. No, sir.
Q. What is your post office address? A. Catoosa, I. T.
Q. Are all the persons named in the application now living? A. Yes, sir.
Q. Is their post office address the same as yours? A. Yes, sir.
Q. Do the persons you represent live with you on the home place? A. Yes, sir.
Q. Do you own a home of your own in the Creek Nation? A. Yes, sir.
Q. Have you already selected that home place? A. Yes, sir.

Q. For whom did you select it? A. For myself.

Q. Are the persons named in this application in possession of the lands named opposite of their names? A. Yes, sir.

Q. You make application for your grandson, David Nero, for the north east quarter of section 35, township 19, range 15, is that correct? A. Yes, sir.

Q. Are there any improvements on that tract of land? A. No, sir.

Q. Does anyone else claim this land or any portion of it? A. No, sir.

Q. Has anyone else any improvements on it? A. No, sir.

Q. Do you know where this land is? A. Yes, sir.

Q. Have you seen it and been over it? A. Yes, sir.

Q. Have you examined it with a view to making application for it? A. Yes, sir.

Q. Is it prairie or timber land? A. Timber land.

Q. You also make application for your daughter Minnie Davis for the north west quarter of the south west quarter of section 36, and the north half of the south east quarter of section 35, township 19, range 15, is that correct? A. Yes, sir.

Q. Are there any improvements on that tract of land? A. No, sir.

Q. Does anyone else claim this land or any portion of it? A. No, sir.

Q. Has anyone else any improvements on it? A. No, sir.

Q. Do you know where this land is? A. Yes, sir.

Q. Have you seen it and ben [sic] over it? A. Yes, sir.

Q. Have you examined it with a view to making this application for it? A. Yes, sir.

Q. Is it prairie or timber land? A. Timber land.

Q. Are each of these tracts of land suitable for homes for the persons for whom they are herein designated? A. Yes, sir.

Q. Is it your intention to make homes for them for your daughter and your grandchild? A. Yes, sir.

Q. Are you making these applications in good faith in all respects? A. Yes, sir.

Q. Will you accept these lands as final allotments for the persons named in this application? A. Yes, sir.

Q. Are there any churches, school-houses, court-houses or burial grounds on this land?

A. No, sir.

Witnesses:
John G. Leiber(?)
R. R. Cravens

Anderson (his X mark) <u>Davis</u>

> Subscribed and sworn to before me this 12th day of September, 1899 at Muscogee, Indian Territory.
>
> Commission expires, Dec. 18, 1902
> John G. Leiber (?)
> Notary Public

Lucinda's Story

More can be learned about Lucinda Davis and her life story because she was interviewed in the 1930s as part of the WPA Slave Narrative project. Her interview is one of the most outstanding of the narratives because of the history and culture that she described in her interview. Though not sure of her birthplace, she was born in the Creek Nation, and her parents were enslaved by Opothleyaholo. But she was separated from her parents, as she was sold to an old Creek man, Tuskaya-hiniha.

She begins with a reference to small poems that she recited in English. She pointed out that she learned the poems after she became an adult, because she did not learn English until she was an adult. She must have spoken with a heavy Muscogee accent, because it is clear that English was not her mother tongue. She begins with a reference to the poems.

> And I think I learn both of dem long after I been grown, 'cause I belong to a full-blood creek Indian and I didn't know nothing but Creek talk long after de Civil War. My mistress was part white and knowed English talk, but she never did talk it because none of de people talked it. I heard it sometime, but it sound like whole lot of wild shoat in de cedar brake scared at something when I do hear it. Dat was when I was little girl in time of de War.
>
> I don't know where I been born. Nobody never did tell me. But my mammy and pappy git me after de Ar and I know den whose chile I is. De men at de Creek agency hep em git me, I reckon, maybe.
>
> First thing I remember is when I was a little girl and I belong to old Tuskaya-hiniha. He was big man in the Upper Creek, and we have a purty good size farm, jest a little bit to de north of the wagon depot houses on de old road at Home Springs. Dat place was about twenty-five mile south of Fort Gibson, but I don't know nothing about whar de fort is when I was a little girl at dat time, I know de Elk River 'bout two miles north of whar we live, cause I been dere many de time.

She describes the status of Tuskaya-hiniha within the Creek Nation. He was a man of stature among the Upper Creeks, and she provided much detail about her life with Tuskaya-hiniha. He had a daughter whose husband had died, who was living with them. The old man's daughter Luwina had given birth to a baby, and Lucinda, while still a child herself, was purchased to look after the child.

> Luwina had a little baby boy and dat de reason old Master buy me, to look after de little baby boy. He didn't have no name 'cause he wasn't big enough when I was with dem, but he git a name later on, I reckon. We call him "Istidji," that mean "little man."
>
> When I first remember before the War old Master had 'bout as many slaves as I got fingers, I reckon. I can think dem off on my fingers like did, but I can't recollect de names.

She described her life as a slave to old Tuskaya-hiniha in detail. He was old and his eyesight had begun to fail. During that time, as his vision worsened, some of the other slaves began to slip away and seize their own freedom. She goes on in her interview, where she describes her life as a young girl with no childhood, whose task it was to tend to other children. Another one of her tasks was to lead the old man around, because of his failing eyesight.

She also describes when there was clearly resistance to enslavement as some of the slaves were beginning to escape when the opportunity presented itself.

> Dey call all de slaves "Istilusti." Dat mean "Black man."
>
> Old man Tuskaya-hiniha was near 'bout blind before de War, and 'bout time of de War he go plumb blind and have to set on de long seat under de bresh shelter of de house all de time. Sometime I lead him around de yard a little, but not very much. Dat about de time all de slave begin to slip out and run off.

Her narrative is important because she had such excellent recall about the families that lived in the Creek community where she was a child. Her descriptions of her life are infused with the Muscogee language that was her mother tongue.

> My own pappy was name Stephany. I think he take dat name 'cause when he little his mammy call him "Istifani." Dat mean a skeleton, and he was a skinny man. He belong to de Grayson family and I think his master name George, but I din't know. Dey big people in de Creek, and with de white folks too. My mammy was Serena and she belong to some of the Gouge family. Dey was big people in de Upper Creek, and one de biggest men of the Gouge was Hopoethleyoholo for his Creek name. He was a big man and went to the North

> in de War and died up in Kansas, I think. Dey say when he was a little boy he was called hopoethli which mean "good little boy" and when he git grown he make big speeches and dey stick on the "yoholo." Dat mean "loud whooper."

Her interview also provides a glimpse into life in a small Creek settlement, including naming practices. In addition, she mentions that something about the status of her parents changed, as they obtained freedom, which unfortunately did not affect her own status. So she as a child was still enslaved and separated from her parents. Her childhood consisted of tending to the young grandchild of her slave master.

> Maybe my pappy and mammy run off and git free, or maybeso dey buy demselves out, but anyway, dey move away some time and my mammy's master sell me to old man Tushkaya-hinihi when I was jest a little gal. All I have to do is stay in the house and mind the baby.

Growing up as a Creek, and working inside the home, Lucinda learned how to make traditional Creek dishes. She describes many of them, from sofki, a traditional Creek dish, to other methods of making corn-based dishes.

> Master had a good log house and a bresh shelter out in front like all de houses had. Like a gallery, only it had de dirt for the flo' and bresh for de roof. Day cook everything out in de yard in big pots, and dey eat out in de yard too.
>
> Dat was sho' good stuff to eat, and it make you fat too! Roast de green corn on de ears in de ashes, and scrap off some and fry it! Grind de dry corn, or pound it up and make ash cakes. Den bile de greens—all kinds of greens from out in de woods—and chop up the pork and de deer meat, or de wild turkey meat; maybe all of dem in the big pot at the same time! Fish too, and de big turtle dat lay out on de bank!
>
> Dey always have a pot full of sofki settin right inside de house, and anybody eat when dey feel hungry. Anybody come on a visit always give 'em some of de sofki. If dey don't take none, de old man git mad, too!
>
> When you make de sofki you pound up the corn real fine, den pour in de water an dreen it off to git all de little skin from off'n de grain. Den you let the grits soak and den bile it and let it stand. Sometimes you put in some pounded hickory nut-meats. Dat make it real good.

Lucinda described traditional Creek ways of life, including a description of the tasks of slaves who were weavers are interesting to read. Her descriptions of how people dressed and the rituals practiced at funeral and burial services were quite vivid.

Witness to a Civil War Battle

Lucinda Davis lived close to a major battlefield in the Civil War. She was a near neighbor and practically an eyewitness to the Battle of Honey Springs.[4] She and the old master joined hundreds of others fleeing the battle zone as they headed out onto the Texas Road, going southward to flee the battle. She described seeing the same gray-clothed soldiers fleeing the battle and being pursued by men in blue uniforms in a rapid chase.

> I never forgit de day dat battle of de Civil War happen at Honey Springs! Old Master jest had the green corn all in, and us been having a time gitting it in, too. Jest de women was all dat was left, cause de men slaves had all slipped off and left out. My Uncle Abe done got up a bunch and gone to de North wid dem, but I didn't know den whar he went. He was in dat same battle, and after de War dey called him Abe Colonel. Most all de slaves 'round dat place gone off a long time before dat wid they masters, when dey go wid old man Gouge and a man named McDaniel.
>
> Den jest as we starting to leave here come something across data little prairie sho'nuff! We know dey is Indians de way dey is riding, and de way dey is all strng out. Dey had a flag, and it was all read [red] and had a criss-cross on it dat look lak a saw horse. De man carry it and rear back on it when de wind whip it, but it flap all 'roun de horse's head and de horse pitch and rear lak he know something going to happen sho![5]

The most touching portion of her story was when she was finally retrieved and taken back to her parents from whom she had been separated for so long. She described the men speaking in "English talk" and how she was put on a horse and strapped to the horse to prevent her from falling, and taken to the Creek Agency where she was met by her parents who had been searching for her.

> When we come to de Creek Agency dar is my pappy and my mammy to claim me, and I live wid em in the Verdigris bottom above Fort Gibson till I was grown and dey is both dead. Den I married Anderson Davis at Gibson Station, and we git our allotments on de Verdigris east of Tulsa—kind of south too, close to de Broken Arrow Town.

---

[4] In her narrative, Lucinda Davis mentions her uncle Abe, who "gone to de North wid dem to fight." Abraham Kernell, whom she refers to as Abe Colonel, was enlisted in the 1st Kansas Colored. The unit was created when black men accompanied Opotholey Yohola into Kansas. He did file for and receive a Civil War pension. The unit was later re-designated as the 79th U.S. Colored Infantry, and his pension identifies him as being a soldier in that unit.
[5] This particular part of her narrative describes how she witnessed a Confederate Indian soldier ride up the Texas road with the flag with a "criss-cross" on it. The Gouge estate was extremely close to the battlefield site.

The Honey Springs Battlefield described by Lucinda Davis in her WPA interview.
Courtesy of Oklahoma Historical Society.

There is more to the story of Lucinda Davis. As mentioned before, Lucinda's story is well documented, but the different periods of her life—as a girl, then the years of her marriage, their large family, and their selection of land—have never been presented together. She mentions her children in the interview and that most of her children had died by the 1930s. By presenting her case along with the enrollment cards and land records above, we know a larger part of the story.

Lucinda Davis was a strong Creek woman, and she was a strong African-descended woman. She held strongly to her culture and her mother tongue which was the Muscogee language. We must hope her final days were peaceful. No information has surfaced about her death, but her narrative is one to be shared by many who wish to learn about the lives of those seldom mentioned—those once enslaved in Indian Territory.

Those who wish to know about the customs of Muscogee people will learn a lot from her narrative. Those who wish to read about a woman who was a survivor from a period that brought much pain will grow from reading her story. The details of her life during and after freedom will speak to her resilience and to her fortitude. We should all grow from her strength, and her story.

The Family of Phillip and Elzora Lewis

Many often assume that *all* Indian tribal freedmen were enslaved or children of enslaved people. However, there were people of African ancestry living in Indian Territory before the Civil War who were free people, never enslaved. They were living freely within the Creek Nation, and it must be pointed out that there were many whose mothers were also free born. The case of Phillip and Elzora Lewis is an interesting example.

This family resided in Muskogee, Indian Territory. Both were born about 1869, long after the war had ended, and thus were not born enslaved. Phillip's father belonged to Arkansas town, and there is no indication that his father had ever been enslaved. His mother was enslaved by Roly McIntosh, a well-known name in Creek history. But since his mother had been enslaved, one *might* assume that is why he was put on the Freedmen roll.

His wife Elzora's story was different, as her father was a Choctaw Freedman, which would have had no bearing at all on her status as a Creek. Elzora's mother, Bettie, had been a "free born" woman, and thus should have made her eligible to be considered or treated differently, and *not* as a woman once enslaved.

Sadly the concept of treating those of African ancestry differently was accepted as being something normal in Indian Territory as in other parts of the slave-holding South. Such treatment was considered appropriate, as it still is among some of the tribes today. And of course the race-based policies of the Dawes Commission prevailed, and the tribes continued to embrace these southern policies. Therefore Elzora was placed on the Dawes roll as a "freedman" even though her mother was a free woman living as a Creek.

It is often said that a child follows the status of the mother, yet clearly Elzora's mother was Creek, lived as a Creek, and belonged to a Creek town. But—as is evidenced on the Enrollment Card—she was classified as a Creek Freedman instead of Creek by Blood.[6]

Application Jacket

Unfortunately, there is no Dawes Interview packet for the Lewis family. Within the Creek nation, many of the Dawes interviews are "missing" and simply not found among the microfilmed records. However,

---

[6] The status of her mother is reflected on the second image—the reverse side of the enrollment card.

thankfully there is much more to learn about the Lewis family, and in fact, a far *better* interview with Elzora is found in the Western History Collection at the University of Oklahoma.

Front of Creek Enrollment Card #105.

Back of Creek Enrollment Card #105.

In January of 1937, Elzora was interviewed by the team working for the Indian Pioneer History project. Those interviews are part of the Western History Collection of the University of Oklahoma, and they are also digitized and online. Elzora's story is found in these records. Because she was able to speak freely, her interview was wonderfully rich with data about her family with more information than the Dawes interview, wherever it might be, would contain.

Her life story and that of her parents is an amazing one. Her mother was the daughter of Rolla Scott, a Creek who came to the Territory quite early. Elzora even had information about her father's parents—her grandparents, some of whom were reluctant to remove to the Territory, and she went into detail about them in her narrative.[7]

ELZORA L. (FULSOM) LEWIS
Route 1, Box 58
Muskogee, Oklahoma
Interview - June 29 1937
Jas S. Buchanan, Field Worker
Indian-Pioneer History.

I (Elzora Lewis) was born July 29, 1871 at Muskogee, I. T.

My father, Louis Fulsom, was a Choctaw Freedman. Little was known of his parents. His father's name was Yak Fulsom and mother was Maria Fulsom.

My mother was Elizabeth Scott Fulsom, the daughter of Rolla Scott, a Creek Indian who settled in the Creek Nation when the Five Civilized Tribes moved to the Indian Territory. Four years of his early manhood were spent in one of the northern states where he learned to speak the English language fluently and became an interpreter on his return to the Indian Territory, at a point then known as South Canadian.

Susie (Bruner) Scott, wife of Rolla Scott, maternal grandmother of Elzora Fulsom Lewis, refused to come to the Indian Territory with her husband Rolla Scott, as she was a free Negro of mixed Indian blood and feared being made a slave if once she left her immediate family circle. Later she came to the Indian Territory with her parents Joe and Delia Bruner. Delia Bruner died during their long journey to the Indian Territory. In later years, after coming to the Indian Territory, Susie Bruner became the trusted treasurer of J. S. Murrow of the Bacone College at Muskogee.

Joe Bruner was a Creek interpreter in the service of the U.S. government.

I received my academic training in a Baptist Missionary School located on Agency Hill where the veteran's hospital now stands on Honor Heights. The old

---

[7] Western History Collection, University of Oklahoma, Indian Pioneer Project, WPA Interview with Elzora (Fulsom) Lewis, June 28, 1933, Interview #6432.

stone building now used as an Indian museum, built to house the Indian agency of the Five Civilized Tribes, and later abandoned, was used as a dormitory and administration building by this by the Creek Mission school when it was established.

This school was established by Robert A. Lesley, a Creek Indian, for the training of Negro Freedmen children.

Ana Lesley, the wife of Rev. Lesley was a Negro and educated in the east. Her services were invaluable in the training of the students at the Evangel Mission, as the school was known.

Associated with the school was also J. S. Murrow of the Bacone College.

This mission later became one of the free tribal schools for Creek Freedmen.

May 24, 1889, I was married to Phillip A. Lewis, Creek Freedman. To this union were born three children. A son, who died in infancy, and two daughters, Edna Lewis Fuller and Melvina Lewis Ward. Our grandchildren are Posetta Ward and Edneil [sic], Fairfax Neely, and Joe Fuller.

Elzora points out that she attended a "Baptist Missionary School located on Agency Hill, on Honor Heights in Muskogee." People in the city of Muskogee, who are familiar with Honor Heights know that this was the site of the former school for Creek children which was known as Evangel Mission. This building is today known as the Five Civilized Tribes Museum. On the grounds of the museum there are several historical markers reflecting its history. Unfortunately, as of 2020, there is no marker pointing out the history of Evangel Mission School.

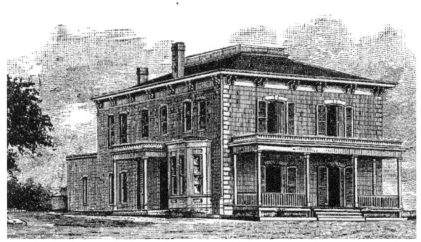

**Evangel Mission is now the home of the Five Civilized Tribes Museum, in Muskogee, OK.
Image from a letterhead of Evangel Missions School stationery.**

In the interview Elzora Lewis provided information about the school's history, and she also mentions the names of some of the founders and people of influence who supported the school and who also taught in the school. In her interview we learn more about her family, because Elzora mentioned not only her children, but also her grandchildren who would have still been living in Muskogee at the time. We hope that their descendants are now aware of their rich history that has been well documented from multiple sources.

Elzora's Father—A Choctaw Freedman

From the Choctaw Nation, but also living the Creek nation, was Elzora's father Louis Folsom. He was admitted by the commission as a Choctaw Freedman. His own card can be found on Choctaw Enrollment Card #466. His parents were Yap Colbert and Lydia Colbert. His parents were enslaved by Pittman Colbert, whereas he himself had been enslaved by Sampson Folsom.

It should also be pointed out that Louis Folsom had four additional Creek Freedmen children who are listed on Creek Enrollment Card #360 on Field Card Number 370. They all reside in Checotah, in the Chambers household. It is common to find that many families living in Indian Territory had close family members who were enrolled in a different tribe. The inter-connected families lived among each other, and shared customs, culture and traditions. Like Louis Folsom, many individuals lived with the community of another nation.

Front of Choctaw Enrollment Card #466.

Within Louis Folsom's Dawes packet are several interesting pages. There is an interview with him, and also an interview with one of his grown children, as well. His own interview was simple and forthright, and cleared him through the Dawes enrollment process. And like many Freedmen he had to provide "proof" of his claims to being a citizen of a particular tribe. The "proof" was often testimony of another person under oath, confirming the truth of what the applicant was stating. Louis Folsom's application testimony is included starting on the next page.

Back of Choctaw Enrollment Card #466.

In the matter of the application of Louis Folsom to the Commission to the Five Civilized Tribes, at Goodland, I. T., May 8th 1899, for enrollment as a Chickasaw Freedman. Being duly sworn by Commissioner Needles, and examined by him et. al., he testified as follows:

Q. What is your name? A. Louis Folsom.
Q. How old are you? A. I was born in 1837.
Q. Who was your owner? A. Sampson and Kitty Folsom.
Q. Where have you lived since you were turned loose? A. I stayed here two years and then went to the Creek Nation. I am married and have a Creek woman.
Q. You live in the Creek Nation, now, do you? A. Yes, sir.
Q. And your children are Creeks are they? A. Yes, sir.
Q. Is there anybody here that know that you belonged to Folsom? A. Yes sir, lots of them.

Foster Shoals being duly sworn testifies as follows:

Q. What is your name? A. Foster Shoals.
Q. Do you know Louis Folsom? A. Yes, sir.
Q. How long have you known him? A. All his life, he was raised there with me.
Q. Who was his master? A. Sampson Folsom.

> Q. How long did he stay here after the war before he went off? A. I don't know exactly how long.
>
> (Enrolled Louis Folsom as Chickasaw Freedman)[8]

Because the structure of this family is complex, all the pages in this fairly lengthy file should be examined. There are twenty-six pages in the application jacket of Louis Folsom alone that are rich with data. Another interview found in the file is with an adult daughter Lizzie. This daughter would have been a half-sister to Elzora Lewis. She was questioned about her father, and though she could not answer some of the questions about him, she was still enrolled on the same card with him.

An interesting handwritten note also appears in the Dawes enrollment packet verifying the history of Louis Folsom, Elzora's father. Individuals who knew him since birth testified that he was indeed born where he stated that he was and that he had truly lived in the stated community. It should be pointed out that at the time of the Dawes interview, Louis Folsom was in his sixties, which makes these handwritten sworn statements even more amazing and important. In that letter, the three people quoted were able to provide the exact birthdate for Louis Folsom, Elzora Lewis's father. He was born in 1837, and those who signed the letter knew him from his earliest years.

The family history of Elzora Lewis's family is a rich one, and it shows how interconnected many of the Freedmen families were. Their families often overlapped with citizens of other tribes. The Freedmen were aware of their histories and were able to prove who they were. Elzora and her family were strongly Creek in culture, lifestyle, and identity. However, her father and half-siblings were Choctaw Freedmen.

As stated earlier, in Elzora's interview with the Indian Pioneer project, she spoke about her education at Evangel Mission School.[9] The building that once housed the school is now the Five Civilized Tribes Museum in Muskogee, Oklahoma.[10] This is a wonderful example of a rich family legacy, and we also hope that the descendants of Lizzie Williams as well as Elzora Lewis someday met, or will meet and can appreciate their shared history.

---

[8] This interview was included because of the relationship between Freedmen in other tribes. Louis Folsom was not Creek, but in fact Choctaw. And interestingly, when the interview was prepared by the stenographer, it was stated on the official interview that he was enrolled as Chickasaw when he was, in fact actually Choctaw. His name appears on the final rolls as a Choctaw Freedman.

[9] More on Evangel Mission can be gleaned from the African-Native American blog where a detailed article about the school's history appears. The article is found at: https://african-nativeamerican.blogspot.com/2011/07/evangel-mission-school-for-creek.html

[10] The Five Civilized Tribes Museum is located on Honor Heights in Muskogee, and the museum is still operating today. See their website: www.fivetribes.org.

Indian Territory }
Kiamichia Co. }

    Before me, J.P. Moreland, a Notary Pub-
lic in and for Kiamichia Co. Ind. Ter., on this day
Personally appeared Charles Williams, Mose Folsom,
and Rhodie Homer, who being by me duly
sworn upon oath says: We have known
Louis Folsom all his life, he was born at
Doaksville I.T., in December a.d. 1837, his
Parents moved from Doaksville to "the Big Farm"
near Grant I.T. where Mose Folsom lived until
Freed, he there remained there until the
year of 1866, when he moved near old Goodland I.T.
and worked for Peter Matubby and Jim Colbert
during the year of 1866, and in the early part
of the year of 1867 he moved back to Doaksville I.T.
and after living there a short time, he left and
went to the Creek Nation, where he lived up to
the year 1899, when he moved back to his old
Home near Grant I.T. where he now lives.

Witness:

Hubbard Babb

W.J. Chester.

Charles his x mark Williams

Mose his x mark Folsom

Rhodie her x mark Homer

Subscribed and sworn to before me, the 14th day of Nov. a.d. 1903
          J.P. Moreland   Notary Public
    Commission expires oct. 31 - 1905

Notarized Statement from Lewis Folsom's folder.

Fannie Rentie Bumpus and Family

Fannie Rentie has an amazing history. She was the daughter of Pickett and Mary Rentie, and during her lifetime she was known by multiple names. Among her surnames were Rentie, Chapman, Island, Bumpus, and Ensley. In spited of her multiple names and records in scattered places, her story is still a rich one to tell.

On her Dawes enrollment card, nothing appears to be very complicated about her story. Her personal data is recorded on Creek Freedman Field Card number 584. She appeared in front of the Dawes Commission in 1898 for herself and her children, Alice and George. Alice would later pass away before the enrollment process was completed. Her husband at the time was Willis Bumpus, father of the two children.

Front of Creek Freedman Field Card #584.

Fannie lived in the town of Boynton, and belonged to Canadian colored Town. Her husband was not Creek, and as was indicated on her card, he was a U.S. citizen. In many parts of Indian Territory U.S. citizens were sometimes referred to as "state" men or "state Negroes." She had once been enslaved by Sukey Kernal, and in the post-Civil War years, she had been enrolled on the Dunn Roll. At that time she was enrolled as Fannie Rentie, with the surname used by her parents, Pickett and Mary Rentie. Both of her parents had also once been enslaved by Sukey Kernal, and they, like Fannie, belonged to Canadian town, and in addition, both parents had their names listed on the Dunn Roll after the Civil War.

Back of Creek Freedman Field Card #584.

Additional Information

Unfortunately, as members of the Creek Nation, the data one would expect to obtain from the application jackets simply does not exist, so we lack information that is available for other tribes. Nevertheless, much more can be learned about Fannie. There were numerous documents in the file, including records showing the exact location of the land with the legal descriptions of the land.

Thankfully, the Land Allotment jackets in Fannie's case filled a void in the family's narrative. For example, she had, during her lifetime, several surnames, and the issue about her many surnames can be found in the Land Allotment records packet. In addition, there were numerous interviews about the land she was to receive, the condition of the land, improvements upon it and more. In 1903, when she was being interviewed regarding her selection of land, she was then Fannie Ensley. There was much discussion about her parcel of land. She was making a selection for her daughter Alice who had not yet passed away. Also present was Thomas Ensley, who was at that time her husband.[11]

---

[11] Ancestry.com. *Oklahoma and Indian Territory, Land Allotment Jackets for Five Civilized Tribes, 1884-1934.* [database online]. Provo, UT, USA: Ancestry.com Operations, Inc, 2014.

DEPARTMENT OF THE INTERIOR
COMMISSION TO THE FIVE CIVILIZED TRIBES
MUSKOGEE LAND OFFICE
MUSKOGEE, I. T., FEBRUARY 24TH 1903

IN THE MATTER OF THE APPLICATION OF Fannie Ensley—nee Bumpus—to take an allotment of land in the Creek Nation for her daughter, Alice Bumpas, accompanied by a proper description of land applied for and a certificate showing that she has been listed for enrollment as a citizen of said Nation.

FANNIE ENSLEY, nee Bumpas being first duly sworn by John G. Lieber, notary public testified as follows:

Q. What is your name? A. Fannie Ensley now. I was on the roll as Fannie Bumpus.

Q. What is your post office address? A. Lee.

Q. Are you a citizen of the Muskogee Nation? A. Yes, sir.

Q. For whom do you make application for allotment? A. My daughter Alicy Bympus [*sic*].

Q. Is Alice living and living with you at this time? A. Yes, sir.

Q. Is she a citizen of the Muskogee Nation? A. Yes, sir.

Q. To what town does she belong? A. Canadian.

Q. Is your name on the Dunn Roll. A. Yes, sir.

Q. How long has Alice lived in the Creek Nation? A. All her life.

Q. Has she been out of the territory in the last four years? A. No, sir.

Q. Does she own a home in the Creek Nation? A. No, sir.

Q. You make application for your daughter Alice Bumpus for the west half of the south west quarter of the south east quarter; the south half of the north west quarter of the south east quarter; the east half of the east half of the south east quarter of the south west quarter; and the west half of the north east quarter of the south east quarter, and the west half of the east half of the north east quarter of the south east quarter of Section 33, Township 14, Range 9, containing 80 acres is that correct? A. Yes, sir, I guess it is. I have not seen this land. This is my husband here with me. He selected this land for me.

Q. Are you willing for your husband having been over and selected land for allotment to Alice? A. Yes, sir.

THOMAS ENSLEY being first duly sworn by John Lieber, notary public, testified as follows:

Q. What is your name? A. Thomas Ensley.

Q. Are you the husband of Fannie Ensley, nee Bumpus, the applicant herein? A. Yes, sir.

Q. Are you familiar with the above described land? A. Yes, sir.

Q. Are there any improvements on this land? A. No, sir.

Q. Is there a house on it? A. No, sir.

Q. Does anyone else claim this land or any part of it? A. No, sir, not that I know of.

Q. Have you been over and examined this land with a view to assisting to making application for it? A. Yes, sir.

Q. Is it prairie or timber land? A. Timber land.

Q. Is this land suitable for a home for Alice? A. Yes, sir.

Q. Are there any churches, school houses, court-houses or burial grounds on this land? A, No, sir.

FANNIE ENSLEY, (nee Bumpus) recalled, testified as follows:

Q. Do you accept this land for Alice Bumpus as her final land allotment in the Creek Nation? A. Yes, sir.

Fannie Ensley
Thomas Ensley
FANNIE ENSLEY, (NEE BUMPUS) FOR HER DAUGHTER ALICE BUMPUS

Subscribed and sworn to before me, this the 24th day of February, A. D., at Muskogee, Indian Territory.

John G. Lieber, NOTARY PUBLIC

In addition, more interesting details about Fannie and her parents and their lives within Creek culture and community are found in her interview made in the 1930s as part of the Indian Pioneer Project. She was interviewed in 1937, and she told fascinating aspects of her life. She made several references to old communities that had ceased to exist in the 1930s, including Old Agency. By that time she used the name Chapman. Her interview with the Pioneer Project follows below. It is found among the 116 volumes of oral histories found in the Western History Collection at the University of Oklahoma.[12]

---

[12] Ancestry.com. *Oklahoma and Indian Territory, Land Allotment Jackets for Five Civilized Tribes, 1884-1934.* [database on-line]. Provo, UT, USA: Ancestry.com Operations, Inc, 2014.

FANNIE (RENTIE) CHAPMAN, Informant. Creek freedman
Route 3, Box 2730
Muskogee, Oklahoma
April 14 -37
Jas A. Buchanan

I was born January 1856 in the Creek Nation near Snake Creek a few miles southwest of where the town of Leonard is now situated. I was one of eleven children born to Pickett and Mary Rentie, who were both born in Alabama in slavery and was owned by a wealthy Creek woman "Dycey [?] Barnwell," and her husband was a white man. I remember my parents telling me of the movement of the Creeks in 1836 and of the sinking of a steam boat that was just ahead of the boat they were on during the trip, while on the Mississippi, and drowning many Indians and slaves.

Ycey [?] Barnwell settled on the above mentioned location and cultivated much land and also had a house north of where Muskogee now stands, between Muskogee and the Arkansas River, and she was residing at this place when the civil war broke out, and she with my parents and family move[d] to hear farm on Snake Creek where we remained until after the war was over. After the war and my parents were free people, my father took up a claim between where Muskogee is now located and the Arkansas River, in the vicinity now known as the Helmer school and it was on this old place that we children grew to maturity and I was married in 1875 to James Island a Seminole Indian, who died in 1893. No children were born to that union. Later I was married to Roff Chapman, a colored non-citizen farmer who died a few years later.

When the Creek allotments were made, I drew my allotment of 160 acres three miles north of Boynton, where I always made my home until 1933 when I was finally swindled out of my property by loan companies, individuals and people in whom I had misplaced confidence. When we children were all at the old home place north of Muskogee, the settlers who were our neighbors were the Bemo family who lived west of us about two miles, Uncle Jess Franklin who lived just west of the Bemo place and Simon Brown who was a freedman, and his place joined the Bemo place on the east. All the government Indian affairs were transacted at that time at the old Creek agency which was located near Fern Mountain.[13]

---

[13] "Interview with Fannie Rentie Chapman." The University of Oklahoma Western History Collection, Digital Collections, Indian Pioneer Collection, Volume 17.

As mentioned earlier, her land allotment file was full of data, as there was much controversy about her right to certain parcels of land. At the end of her interview she makes mention of the fact that she lived on her land for many years, but later lost the land.

The descendants of Fannie Rentie Bumpus, (also known as Chapman and Ensley), are strongly encouraged to obtain the allotment application file. Dozens of pages are contained pertaining not only to the land itself, but also to the various husbands Fannie had and the names she used when some of the land transactions occurred.

Fannie's interview for the Indian Pioneer project will take the reader more deeply into the life of late nineteenth-century pre-Oklahoma life. And the interview speaks vividly to multiple aspects of life within the Creek Nation, for Freedmen as well as for all individuals living near Muskogee and the now vanished community of Old Agency.

In 1940, Fannie Chapman was still living in the Muskogee area.[14] Her name was recorded in the 1940 census, and she was living in the household of Elmer Byers. She is listed as a housekeeper along with her son George and grandson George Bumpus Jr. Hopefully their legacy prevails and the family can still celebrate a fascinating history.

1940 Federal Census, reflecting Fannie Chapman and family.

---

[14] Federal Census, 1940; Oklahoma, Muskogee County, Muskogee Township, Enumeration District 51-54, Sheet 14B.

The Life and Times of Hagar Myers

Hagar Myers.
Courtesy of Lesa Myers Engram.

Found among the many records of the Creek Freedmen, the history of the Myers family of Muskogee is deeply rooted in the Creek Nation. For John Myers, the head of the house, the story is a complex one, because unlike many who were classified as Creek Freedmen, John Myers' own roots are not among that of the enslaved. He was born free, as were his parents Harris and G. A. G. Myers. They were among many free-born people of African descent who lived among the Muscogee Creek people. Despite their being free African Creeks, their entire identity would eventually be placed in "second class" status as "freedmen," though they as free people never needed to be "freed."

However, John Myers' wife, Hagar, was born enslaved by Sukey Kernal, as was Hagar's mother, Diana. It was decided conveniently that because of Hagar's status as having once been enslaved, that the entire family would then be classified as having been enslaved, and thus recognized as "freedmen." This policy would place the entire family under a "badge" of slavery, thus marking them as different, despite other factors that made them Creeks in heritage, lifestyle, language, and culture.

The family resided in the Muskogee area, and they belonged to North Fork Town. Both had also previously been placed on the Dunn Roll. Hagar's father, Harris, belonged to Arkansas town, and her mother belonged also to North Fork town. A previous name of the family was Hardage, as noted on the back of the enrollment card.

Front of Creek Enrollment Card #1057, Field Card #1083.

Back of Creek Enrollment Card #1057, Field Card #1083.

In September of 1898, they appeared in front of the Dawes commission in application as Creek citizens. Though free and never enslaved, John and his mother Harriet, also born free, were still placed on the rolls of Freedmen, of the Creek Nation. Harriet, John's mother was still living at the time and was placed on the same card. Note that her mother's name appears as Harris on one line and a Harriet on the same card. Also the names as they appeared on the earlier Dunn Roll, taken in 1867 was also reflected on the back of the Dawes card.

Harriet, John's mother, was seventy years old at the time she appeared before the Commission, and her parents were identified on the card. Her father was John (Jno.) Cooney who died during the Civil War. Harriet's mother's name was Dorcas Hardage. Note also that Dorcas was at one time enslaved by Siah Hardridge.

The front of the card clearly says that Harriet was free, but it is not certain how Harriet became a free person. On the back of the card, the notes say that her mother, at least, had been enslaved. It was usually common practice that the status of one born in slavery or one being free was determined by the status of the mother. But the card clearly indicates that Harriet was not enslaved by anyone in the Creek Nation. So her free status is not clear. Possibly she was manumitted in the years before removal to Indian Territory. By Harriet's age, it is clear that she was born before the removal of Creeks to Indian Territory, so her freedom was gained in the early 1800s.

Additional information

Like many Creek families there are many challenges that pertain to researching them, due to numerous missing interviews that were never captured when the records were microfilmed. But thankfully, many gaps in the family narrative can be filled by studying the land records, and the researcher may not only determine where land allotments were, but also fill in some of the missing story. Note the following interview from the land allotment application jacket.

INTERIOR DEPARTMENT
COMMISSION TO THE FIVE CIVILIZED TRIBES.
MUSCOGEE LAND OFFICE, Sep. 23, 1899

In the matter of the application of Harriet Walker (represented by her son, John Myers) for allotment as a citizen of the Creek Nation, accompanied by proper description of the lands applied for, and certificate that she is entitled to take under the rules of the Secretary of the Interior, and being sworn by Acting Chairman Bixby, testifies as follows:

Q. What is your name? A. John Myers.
Q. Are you the son of Harriet Walker the applicant? A. Yes
Q. Do you make this filing for her at her instance [sic] and request? A. Yes
Q. Is your mother, Harriet Walker, a citizen of the Muskogee Nation? Yes.
Q. Is her name on the Dunn Roll? A. Yes.

Q. What town does she belong to? A. North Fork Colored.

Q. How long has she lived in the Creek Nation? A. Ever since I can recollect, and I am about 44.

Q. Has she been outside the Indian Territory in the last two years? A. No.

Q. What is your post office address? A. Muscogee.

Q. Is your mother now living? A. Yes.

Q. Does she own a home of her own in the Territory? A. No.

Q. Is she in actual possession of the lands named in this application which you wish to select for her? A. Yes.

Q. Are there any improvements on that land? A. Yes.

Q. Is there a house on it? A. Yes.

Q. Who lives in the house? A. We do.

Q. How many acres are there under cultivation on that land? A. About 23 acres.

Q. Is the improved land fenced? A. Yes, sir.

Q. Does anyone else claim this land or any portion of it? A. No.

Q. Has anyone else any improvements on this land? A. No, sir.

Q. Do you know where this land is? A. Yes.

Q. Have you seen this land and been over it? A. Yes.

Q. Have you examined it with a view to making this application for it? A. Yes.

Q. Is it prairie or timbered land? A. A little timber and part prairie.

Q. Is this land suitable for a home for your mother? A. Yes.

Q. Do you make this application in good faith in all aspects? A. Yes.

Q. Will you accept this land as the final allotment of your mother in part? A. Yes.

Q. Are there any churches, school-houses, court-houses, or burial grounds on this land? A. No.

John Myers

Sworn and testified before me this the 23rd day of Sep. 1899,

Tams Bixby[15]

---

[15] The land records for the Meyers family are basically standard records. General questions were asked pertaining to the family members, the description of the land, as well as to whether there were any improvements upon the land. These records can be viewed in depth online via Ancestry.com, and also on Family Search.

Hagar's Story and the Green Peach War

Hagar's family can be found on the Dawes records and the Dunn Roll for Creek Freedmen. However, a wonderful gem was found about Hagar Meyers in the Western History Collection of the University of Oklahoma. In the case of Hagar Meyers we have an unusual story associated with this woman from a time of conflict. It was she who is credited with providing critical information during the Green Peach War which led to a peaceful end to the conflict. As a result, she is a woman whose history should not be forgotten.

Her actions are described in a fascinating interview that became part of the Indian Pioneer Project. The person being interviewed was Scott Waldo McIntosh, one of the sons of William McIntosh, who provided this amazing story of Hagar Myers. According to McIntosh, Hagar Myers, a Creek freed woman, was possibly the one person responsible for bringing peace during the Green Peach War.

McIntosh describes how, during the time of the conflict known as the Green Peach War, there was a need to get a message to Isparecher (Spieche) that soldiers were being dispatched from Fort Gibson. If they did not surrender peacefully, a massacre would surely have occurred. This is where Hagar's story emerges.[16]

...While Spieche and his forces were in the Sac and Fox country, a message was desired to be delivered by the women of the Loyal Creeks to Spieche to notify him of the coming of the soldiers from Fort Gibson. It was their desire that he surrender without resistance, but how could they get the message through? No man could get through the lines of the Checote Army and possibly not a woman. One woman, Hager Meyers who lives today four miles west of Muskogee, Oklahoma, on Highway 62 and 64, near Memorial Park Cemetery, shouted out, "I'll go carry the message to surrender. If I get through well enough, if not, then I have done my all and the best I know to do, to save further bloodshed, for a few dollars due each of us." She was furnished the best horse they had, and started for the Sac and Fox agency. She was stopped many times but by her cunning ways, and ideas and many falsehoods she reached Spieche and delivered the message. The message was read to the rank and file, and the majority shouted "let's all surrender to the blue coats when they get here." Some still held out saying "no, we will die fighting" but the majority always wins and they surrendered as before stated.[17]

Scott Waldo McIntosh gave this interview to the Indian Pioneer Project in the 1930s. He had been a witness to many of the events that had occurred in the nineteenth and early twentieth centuries among the Creeks. The interview, found in its entirety in the Western History Collection of the University of Oklahoma, numbers more than twenty pages. He spoke of many things in his narrative, including the contribution to peace made by this simple woman of courage and conviction.

---

[16] University of Oklahoma, Western History Collection, *Indian Pioneer Papers*. Interview with Scott Waldo McIntosh, Interview Volume 58, #6659.

[17] Excerpt from interview with Scott Waldo McIntosh, Indian Pioneer Project.

Most interestingly, McIntosh also called for Hagar to be honored and remembered for her bravery and that, at the time of her death, a special marker be placed on her grave so her actions would be remembered.

> "Why not appropriate," he said, "a few dollars each month to Hagar Myers who carried the message to Spieche, saving the lives of hundreds of men. If need be, see that she is given at her death a resting place in our National Cemetery at Fort Gibson Oklahoma, in the colored section with a headstone bearing an inscription telling of her service and valor displayed in a great cause.[18]

This part in Hagar's life is notable and is hopefully one to be remembered by many who are students and scholars of Creek history and that of the Green Peach War.

According to the Oklahoma Death index, Hagar Myers died on January 1, 1941. Little is known of her burial site, but it is hoped that the history and legacy of this Creek woman will always be remembered. It is also hoped that the entire Myers family history rooted in both free people as well as in those enslaved by the Creeks will be honored and remembered in future years.

---

[18] Ibid.

The Family of Hester Murphy

In 1899, Hester Murphy applied for herself and her family as citizens of the Creek Nation in front of the Dawes Commission. The records reflect the Murphy family from Coweta, a well-documented family strongly connected to the community, to the land, and to the Muskogee Creek Nation. On the enrollment cards, Hester's name is found, as well as those of her daughters Fannie and Ruth, her sons Fred and Walter, and an associate, Joseph Stephens, who was not related. She was a member of North Fork Town, and prior to the war, was once enslaved by Motey Canard.

Front of Creek Enrollment Card #171.

The following image provides a closer view of the names on the front of the card.

Close-up of Front of Creek Enrollment Card #171.

The enrollment card is full of genealogical data, reflecting not only their names on prior rolls, but also notes on the front of the card reflecting other relationships, such as the spouses of Hester's children and subsequently, their children (Hester's grandchildren) also.

Although Joseph Stephens was not related to Hester, he *did* have a tie to the family. He was listed actually as the father of one of Fannie's children listed on another card.

Close-up view of remarks on Front of Creek Enrollment Card #171.

On the back of the card, we learn that Hester's father had been enslaved by Roley McIntosh, and her mother by Motey Canard. Her father was William Murphy, who was not a Creek citizen.

Printed numbers in first column refer to individual names on reverse side.

	NAME OF FATHER	FATHER'S TRIBAL ENROLLMENT			FATHER'S OWNER	NAME OF MOTHER	MOTHER'S TRIBAL ENROLLMENT			MOTHER'S OWNER
		Year	Town	No.			Year	Town	No.	
1	Ned McIntosh	1890	Arkansas	75	Roley McIntosh	Sarah Canard	Del	Drown Ase	19	Katy Canard
2	Wm Murphy	Del	Non Citizens			No1				
3	" "	"	"			No1				
4	" "	"	"			No1				
5						No1				
6	Father died during Treaty					Phebe Stephens	Del	Arkansas		Watt Grayson
7										
8										
9										
10										
11										
12						Phebe Stephens	no DR	Arkansas	109	Watt Grayson
13										
14										
15										
16										
17										
18										

Back of Creek Enrollment Card #171.

From the Application Jacket

This is one of the rare Creek Freedmen application jackets that is full of data and which contains a very detailed interview. In the interview, attention was directed to Hester's history, how long she had lived in the Territory, and whether or not she was always living in the Creek Nation. She pointed out that she left when "all the people went out." She was referring to the time during the Civil War when many people left their homes to avoid being in the vicinity of the battles and skirmishes.

To verify her presence, several questions were directed to her about various payments made to Creek citizens. They discussed whether she was on the 1890 roll, if she had received the $29 payment, and if she had drawn the $14 that was also paid. Also in the interview the voice of Freedman leader Sugar George was found. He was a major leader who served in the House of Warriors, the House of Kings, and he served as town king of North Fork Colored town.

DEPARTMENT OF THE INTERIOR

Q. What is your name? A. Hester Murphy.
Q. How old are you? A. I guess I am about 46 or 47.
Q. You claim to be a citizen of the Creek Nation? A. Yes sir.
Q. How long have you lived in the Creek Nation? A. I have been here about 16 years, I reckon.
Q. Where were you born? A. Here in the Territory
Q. In the Creek Nation? A. Yes sir, from here about Choska.
Q. Have you been out of the Creek Nation? A. Yes sir.

Q. How long was you gone? A. I couldn't tell exactly how long.

Q. When did you leave? A. Went out when all the people went out.

Q. During the war? A. Yes, sir.

Q. When did you come back? A. I can't remember exactly what time I came back.

Q. Was you here at the time of the Dunn payment when the money was paid out at the old agency by Major Dunn? A. No sir, I can't remember.

Q. Do you think you was here? A. I don't know, sir.

Q. Who did you go out with? A. Went out with a man by the name Barrett.

Q. But don't know when it was? A. No sir, I can't tell you when it was.

Q. Don't know whether you came back before the Dunn payment or not? A. No, sir.

Q. You have been living here now for 15 years? A. 16 or 17 years.

Q. And then came back again? A. Yes, sir.

Q. You were backward and forward several times? A. Yes, sir.

Q. Where did you go? A. To the states.

Q. States? A. Down in Texas.

Q. Your name is on the roll of 1890 is it? A. Yes, sir.

Q. You remember the 29 dollars? A. Yes, sir.

Q. Did you draw the $14? A. Yes sir.

Q. Has your rights ever been questioned? A. No sir.

Q. When you came here 16 or 17 years ago, you then moved away again? A. No sir, I didn't move then, I came on a visit.

Q. The last time you came here permanently to reside was about 11 years ago? A. Yes, sir.

The interview was extensive and quite a fascinating read. Sugar George, a well-known and respected leader in the community, spoke about the Murphy family being at his house. Actually many people ended up camping on the grounds of Sugar George's house right after the war. His place was a well-known gathering place for many finding their way back home into the Creek Nation.

Sugar George had been town king for about twelve years at the time, serving in that capacity since the 1880s. Prior to that time he served in the House of Warriors. As questions were directed to him about the movement of Hester and her family, he pointed out that he knew with certainty that they were back in the Creek Nation before the 1866 treaty was signed. He pointed out that he knew it because he "took them into the yard" when they arrived, and that Hester's family was closely related to him.

SUGAR GEORGE, being sworn and examined, testified as follows:

Q. What is your name? A. Sugar George.

Q. How old are you? A. About 67 years of age.

Q. Where do you live? A. Living on Cane Creek, at Wellington.

Q. How long have you lived in the Creek Nation? A. I have been living in the Creek Nation all the while, all my life time; born in the Creek Nation.

Q. Are you a citizen of the Creek Nation? A. Yes, sir.

Q. Do you know Hester Murphy? A. Yes, sir.

Q. How long have you known her? A. I couldn't say; I couldn't give the length of time; but knowed her since she was a baby.

Q. Do you occupy any official position in the Creek Nation? A. I am senator in the Creek Nation.

Q. King? A. Yes, sir, in the house of Kings.

Q. Town King? A. Of the North Fork, Colored Town.

Q. How long have you been town King? A. It is about 12 years. Before that, I was a warrior; I was changed into a king.[19]

Q. Did you know Hester Murphy's father and mother? A. Yes, well acquainted with them.

Q. What was their name? A. Woman named Sarah Canard, and her father named McIntosh; Ned McIntosh.

Q. Do you know whether Hester Murphy was within the Creek Nation at the time the Major Dunn payment was made at the old agency? A. I don't recollect whether she was or not.

Q. Was she here before the war? A. Yes, sir, she was born in the Creek Nation here, and was here before the war.

Q. Where did she go at the time of the war. A. Her owner carried them down south.

Q. In Texas? A. Yes sir, down in Texas on Red River.

Q. Did you know when Hester returned from the south? A. I actually don't know when she returned

Q. When did her father and mother return? A. I couldn't give the year, but they returned before the '66 treaty; they came in before then.

Q. But Hester didn't come with them, did she? A. I don't know whether she was along or not.

Q. But you do know that her father and mother came back before the treaty of 1866? A. Yes, I knew that very well, because I took them in the yard when they came back; they are a close relation of mine.

Q. Don't you remember whether Hester was with them when they were camping in your yard? A. That I don't recollect exactly.

Q. Do you recollect any of the children Hester's father and mother had at that time, with them? A. I recollect them, but don't recollect whether I could call

---

[19] There were two ruling houses within the Creek Nation at that time, The House of Warriors and the House of Kings. Sugar George served first in the House of Warriors, then later was elected to the House of Kings.

out the names or not.

Q. Did they have some children with them? A. Yes, sir.

Q. How long did the family stay in the Creek Nation after the treaty was concluded?

A. From that on, they were in the nation all the while to my knowing.

Hester took the stand again and when asked about who traveled and returned, she named her family members, including her siblings.

HESTER MURPHY recalled, testified as follows:

Q. Do you remember going to Sugar George's house with your parents? A. Yes, sir.

Q. When you came back from Texas? A. Yes, sir.

Q. How many children were with your father and mother at that time of the children? A. Disa Feta, Anderson, and Elliott

Q. Is that all? A. Yes sir, to my knowing; I don't know how about the older ones whether they were.

Q. You was with them? A. Yes sir, I was there with them.

Q. Where did you go from Sugar George's place? A. Went to where she lived. That was before I went away at all.

Q. Where was that? A. Old Agency.

Q. You said you went to where your parents lived; where was it they lived? A. At old Agency

Q. How long did they live there after that? A. I couldn't tell you that.

Q. You know whether a few months or a few years? A. No sir, I couldn't tell you how long it was.

The third witness was Tacky Grayson, a legislator at that time in the Creek Nation. He was also able to verify Hester's ties to the nation. He knew her parents—her father, Nero McIntosh, and Hester's mother, Sarah. He also corroborated that not only Hester's parents left during the war, but that most people had vacated the area during the war as well. He also confirmed, as did Sugar George, that when peace was declared they were already back in the Creek Nation.

TACKEY GRAYSON, being sworn and examined, testified as follows:

Q. How old are you? A. I was born in 1845, December 25th.

Q. How long have you lived in the Creek Nation? A. All my days,

Q. Are you a citizen of the Muskogee Nation? A. Yes, sir.

Q. Did you ever hold any official position? A. Yes, sir.

Q. What was it? A. A legislator, going on 8 years will be the 5th of December.

Q. Did you know the parents of Hester Murphy? A. Yes sir.

Q. What was her father's name? A. Nero McIntosh.

Q. What was her mother's name? A. Sarah.

Q. Do you know here Ned McIntosh and Sarah were born? A. No sir, they are older than I am; I couldn't tell you that.

Q. Where did you first see them? A. Long after peace was declared I never knowed before peace was declared.

Q. Did you see them before the war? A. I used to know Ned before the war; I knowed Ned and Aunt Sarah before the war.

Q. Do you know whether or not they left this country at the time of the war? A. No sir, but mighty near everybody left the country. But if he left the country and went some place I couldn't tell you.

Q. Did you see them in this country about the time peace was declared? A. Yes, sir.

Q. Do you know whether they were here at the time of the Major Dunn payment? A. At that time, I can't because we didn't keep no record; I remember seeing them here after the war but how lons [sic] I can't go to work and tell the date; if I do I will be a little off; they were her after peace was declared, but used to live around the old agency, and down the point, but just when if I identify it I will be off.

Q. Can't you tell whether they came a year after peace was declared? A. I came here in '66 and saw Ned McIntosh and family. I lived at Red River.

Q. Did you see this girl here at the time? A. I seen the children but never has remembered, if I got to work and tell you and identify that girl; the old lady had a good many children, but my grandmother and that woman's mother were great old cronies, and when they came in before I did, to my recollection, and when I came to the old Creek Agency, but my grandmother came here, names Jennie Grayson, and this old woman and here [sic] like darkeys do have great shake. Sarah said, see sister Jennie have you got your children? She says, I got 13 out; Aunt Sarah says I got all mine; I didn't go to the house; I didn't know the small children and they didn't know me until I became grown; Grandmother says she had 13 out, and Aunt Sarah says she has none out.

Q. Where is your grandmother? A. She's dead.

Document from Hester Murphy Land Allotment File.

Land Allotments

The Murphy family did obtain their land allotments and the allotment records and interviews also tell more of the Murphy family story.[20] Most questions referred to the land and whether it was prairie or timberland. This kind of information can provide a glimpse into the kind of life lived on the land selected by the citizen. Realization that land was timberland or prairie can provide an insight into the tasks facing the family upon settlement onto the new property. Hester was able to select her property without challenge, as were others in her family.

There is much to be learned from the Murphy family file. The relationships that prevailed among the various classes of Creeks were strong, and the Murphys were viewed as Creeks and not as outsiders. However, their status as freedmen—when viewed by the authorities—was outweighed by their simply being viewed and treated as Creek. In addition, the role played by freedmen such as Sugar George was evident; his involvement as a ruler in the nation is verified, and undisputed.

The Murphys, like so many others, endured the turbulence of the Civil War, returned home to the Creek Nation, and reestablished their lives there in the community near the old Agency, and later on their own land. They, like others in the Creek Freedmen community, were closely aligned to all Creeks. The culture of this family was strong and deeply rooted as Muskogee Creek people.

---

[20] Land Allotment Record, Ancestry.com. Provo, UT, USA: Ancestry.com Operations, Inc, 2014.

The Legacy and Story of Phillip A. Lewis

The Lewis family of Muskogee, Oklahoma has already been profiled with a focus on Elzora's side of the family. Phillip and Elzora Lewis applied in front of the Dawes Commission in 1898, and Elzora's family story was outlined in an earlier segment of this work. However, the story of Phillip Lewis is just as detailed, and one can go back even further when examining his family history.

As presented before, the Lewis family resided in Muskogee, and appeared in front of the Dawes Commission in 1898 to enroll themselves and their children as Creek Freedmen. And as in so many other cases, the Application Jackets for this family simply do not exist, were never microfilmed, and have possibly been destroyed or hidden from the public domain. But thankfully a far better interview does exist for Phillip Lewis, and like his wife, Elzora, the Indian Pioneer project in the 1930s provided an opportunity for him to speak freely about his own family history. In addition, the full interview reflected an expansive knowledge of Creek history. A transcription of that interview follows:

PHILLIP A. LEWIS
Route 1, Box 58
Muskogee, Oklahoma
2nd Interview – June 29, '37
Jas. S. Buchanan, Field Worker
Indian-Pioneer History

At the age of 18 I left Tullahassee Mission and went to work for a prominent cattle buyer, of the Indian Territory in those days by the name of Col. Moore. I bought cattle for Col. Moore and delivered them to the Sims Miller ranch on Mingo Creek near Tulsa.

There were no banks in the Territory in those days to handle the financial business for the cattle men, and I have ridden on cattle buying trips with Col. Moore when he would have as much as $5000 in his saddle pockets. I worked for Col. Moore for two years and Mr. Turner. I saved my money and invested it in young cattle when I could get them at a good price and soon established a fair sized herd which I kept on my mother's place which was situated west of where the town of Porter now stands. In 1890 there was a very severe winter which caused the loss of much of my herd.

In 1889, I was married to Elzora Fulsom, the daughter of Lewis and Bettie Fulsom. Two children were born to us as follows:

Edna (Lewis) Fuller, born February 7, 1891
Melvina (Lewis) Ward, born October 24, 1893

Our daughters have been given every educational advantage we could give them. They attended the Lincoln University in Jefferson City Mo. Western University, Quindor Kans., Howard University, Washington D.C. and post courses at Columbia University, New York City N.Y. Melvina, the younger daughter attended the Conservatory of Music in Chicago, finishing in that school.

We lived on a farm until after the girls were of age, and when they were not in school, they were taught to work on the farm. They have helped me break wheat land, making a hand at the plow as well as performing the work of a harvest time or any other work that was to be done.

CREEK PASTURE LAW

In the early '90s the Creek Council passed a law which was known as the "pasture law" which permitted the leasing and fencing of large tracts of pasture lands by large cattle companies and made it prohibitive for a citizen to take a claim on any land that was held under pasture least without the consent of the cattle companies. The rank and file of the Creek people resented this condition and there was much dissatisfaction.

In 1895, I was elected to the Creek legislature on the platform of opposing the pasture law. The influence of the cattle companies prevented the repeal of the pasture law in that session of the legislature. However, there was such protest made against the control of the nation by a few wealthy cattlemen that the newly originated Dawes commission gave this matter their first attention. Due to previous treaties, it was necessary for the Dawes Commission to make a superseding treaty for the abolition of the Creek government, make a complete roll of Creeks and freedmen to determine their citizenship and make allotments of land which would automatically destroy the land monopoly of the cattlemen.

The interview continues, and Phillip Lewis describes how a faction of Creeks resented the pending process of allotment. Some were so opposed to the Dawes allotment process that a larger dissention arose in the nation. He went on to accurately describe how the Dawes Commission was organized, and how Tams Bixby was appointed as the commissioner to the Five Civilized Tribes, and how the process unfolded to distribute allotments of lands. Tams Bixby, he noted made several attempts to meet with the Creek tribal council, but they chose not to meet with him.

As a result, Phillip Lewis wrote a resolution suggesting a joint session of both houses to allow the commission to be heard. He continues to describe this in his interview:

I felt through courtesy to the government, the Commission should be heard. I wrote a resolution recommending a joint session of both houses of the legislature in order that the commission be heard. This resolution was passed, conference arranged and the commission was heard and terminated with gratifying results. During this session a committee was appointed to meet and negotiate a treaty with the government for the purpose in question.

The Dawes Commission was given power to make a tribal roll of all citizens of the Creek Nation. Knowing that many of the citizens were illiterate, I gave my service as council for the Creeks at the Commission headquarters during their registration in order that they might be properly identified to enter their names on the roll.

There was a faction of the Creeks that resented the action of the committee and the agreement with the Commission and were reluctant in registration and through such action many citizens were left off the roll. It was for this reason that I gave my services that all my people would be enrolled. The time spent in this service gave me a fair knowledge of all Freedmen that were entitled to enrollment.

After months of such service, Phillip Hopkins, chief law clerk of the commission asked me by whom I was employed. I informed him that I was not employed by anyone and that I was giving my service in the interest of my people. Mr. Hopkins took the matter up with Mr. Bixby, and had me employed by the government and placed me in full charge of the Colored roll. At the completion of the roll I issued identification cards to each Freedman for their allotment, which completed that service.

Due to the resignation of the superintendent of the Creek orphanage I was appointed to finish his term in 1901. After I was assigned to that position and served about six months, I was transferred to the Tullahassee Mission and placed in charge of the Creek Freedman boarding school.

After serving three years at the Tullahassee Freedman school, I was called to Okmulgee to use my influence with the Creek council in an effort for the ratification of a supplemental treaty with the tribe, which was successfully passed. I then retired to private life.

Phillip A. Lewis

From the interview, some glimpses into the lives of his family can be gleaned. Phillip spent much of his youth in the care of his beloved grandmother Rachel. She was a caregiver to many, and she nurtured many in her Creek community, both while enslaved and after the Civil War. In the post-war years, Rachel continued to care for multiple children even when they were now free and allowed to attend school when of age.

Phillip attended school at Fountain Church for primary education, and later he attended the Tullahassee Manual Labor School for Creek Freedmen. Education was a priority with Phillip, and he became himself an educator, later teaching at the Tullahassee himself.

Tullahassee Manual Labor School.
Courtesy Oklahoma Historical Society.

Phillip Lewis was one of the earliest known freedmen who became an educator at the school he once attended. The Lewis interest in education continued well into the twentieth century. In 1900, he served as superintendent of Evangel Mission School. It was sometimes referred to as the "Creek Colored Orphan Home." The school was founded in 1883, and Lewis served among those who worked at the school. The building today is now the home of the Five Civilized Tribes Museum. It is one of the few landmarks of Freedmen history, although sadly, to date, no historical markers on the grounds reflect its Creek Freedman origins.

1900 Federal Census, Creek Nation, Township 18, Range 18.
This page shows names of students enrolled in the
"Creek Colored Orphan Home," as it was often called.

Letterhead of the Evangel Mission School.

Phillip and Elzora's daughter Melvina worked as a school teacher at an unnamed rural school in the 1920s. In his narrative, Phillip pointed out that they made sure that their daughters were well-educated, sending them to Lincoln, Howard, and Columbia Universities.

The Lewis family lived mostly around the city of Muskogee well into the twentieth century. Phillip and Elzora's names are also found in a city directory for Muskogee, Oklahoma in the mid-1940s.

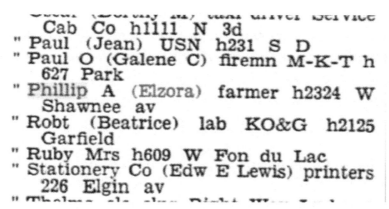

Part of 1920 Federal Census, Muskogee, OK, Ward 4, District 94, showing the entry for Phillip and Elzora Lewis.

U.S. City Directories, 1822-1995, **Muskogee, OK, 1946. Image obtained from Ancestry.com.**

The Grandparents of Phillip A. Lewis

One of the many fascinating features in the narrative of Phillip Lewis was the story of his grandmother Rachel and how she became the wife of King Kernal. The story is more than unusual, because it takes place at a place of sorrow and heartbreak—a slave auction.[21]

Phillip Lewis recounted the story that his grandmother Rachel often told—of how she was being auctioned off to be sold to the highest bidder at a slave auction. One man in the crowd—another enslaved man, in fact—addressed her, and asked if his master purchased her, would she be willing to become his wife.

Thanks to the Indian Pioneer Papers of the Western History Collection, we know of the story of King and Rachel, how they met and how they faced a new life about to unfold for them as they met on the auction

---

[21] Interview with Phillip A. Lewis. University of Oklahoma, Western History Collection. *Indian Pioneer Papers Digital Collection.*

block. This is a rare glimpse of a Native American purchase of an African slave and the story told from the perspective of the enslaved family descendants.[22] In spite of it being a time of heartbreak, the only good thing to emerge from this story was that a degree of love that emerged between the two enslaved people, King and Rachel, and the love that grew from their union endured for decades, through enslavement, into freedom, and to the cusp of statehood.

I recall a story my great grandmother Rachel told to us children many times of how she happened to meet and marry my great grandfather King Kernal. She was a very light mulatto, and stately and a very beautiful woman when she was young, I am sure. King Kernal was a very large man, tall and erect, more than six feet in height, a veritable giant. The story that she would relate was as follows:

When I was only a girl I was taken to a slave market with some other slaves to be sold by a slave trader. Just before the sale my attention was attracted by a large young fellow in the crowd who seemed to never be looking at anyone except me. Finally after working his way closer and closer to me and the opportunity presented itself, he leaned over to me and whispered to me, "If I persuade my master to buy you, will you marry me?" As I looked into his face somehow, something made me say "yes." Without another word, he turned and disappeared into the crowd. He was gone, I was bewildered, lost in a haze of jumbled thoughts. Who was he—to come to me from among the people, the greatest number of people I had ever seen in my life. Why had he said such word, received my answer and disappeared as suddenly and mysteriously as he had came? What did it all mean? I could not understand. Then, I saw him, head and shoulders taller than anyone else, making his way through the crowd in my direction and as he came closer I saw there was another man with him. They came near us and stopped, stood there together looking in my direction and after a short whispered conversation, they approached my master and shortly I was the property of a new master, who was the owner of the man to whom I had given my answer "yes" King Kernal. Our master took King and me to his place and we were married immediately thereafter, though in slavery, we were happy. Our master was kind not to separate us during slavery time, and after we were made free people, only God could separate us.

Truly their family history is a rich one. Phillip's recollection of the story heard from his grandmother takes the family history back to lands east of the Mississippi before removal to the west. This is a rare case where a Freedman family's narrative goes back to the actual slave transaction that took the family westward into Indian Territory.

---

[22] Ibid.

1930 Census, Muskogee Oklahoma, Agency Township, District 3.

Headstone of Phillip A. Lewis,
in Booker T. Washington Cemetery, Muskogee County,
Oklahoma. Image Source: Find a Grave.

Headstone of Elzora Fulsom Lewis,
in Booker T. Washington Cemetery, Muskogee County,
Oklahoma. Image Source: Find a Grave.

The Lewis family thrived well into the twentieth century, with both Phillip and Elzora living into the 1950s. In the 1930 federal census Phillip and Elzora were captured in the census. They were homeowners, and their home was valued higher than most in the community where they lived in Muskogee.

Both Phillip and Elzora saw many changes from the era of slavery, the Civil War, the post-Civil War years in the Creek Nation, to the years of westward expansion, the Dawes Commission era, into statehood and their eventual life as U.S. Citizens. Their history is a rich one, going back over 200 years, and this strongly rooted Oklahoma family has a legacy that is truly an honorable one. The family has a history that should be celebrated. Both Phillip and Elzora are buried in Booker T. Washington Cemetery in Muskogee, Oklahoma.

Minnie Grayson Allen and Family

As challenging as it is to research families from the Creek Nation, it is still worthwhile to explore the records and families presented as part of the Dawes records. One of the many lessons when studying records from Indian Territory is how many people from one nation lived in another part of the Territory, and with Creek Freedmen such was also the case. With Creek citizens one will always see a reference to "tribal towns" which in many cases did not reflect where they lived. One "belonged" to a town while living in another nation's jurisdiction geographically. The case of Minnie Allen is such a case. In this case Minnie Allen was a Creek citizen belonging to North Fork Town, but resided in Stonewall, in another nation entirely.

Front of Creek Enrollment Card #1461, Field Card #1617.

At the time of the Dawes enrollment process, Minnie Grayson Allen resided in the heart of the Chickasaw Nation. She was only twenty-one years of age, and was a member of North Fork Town. Her name had previously been mentioned on the Dunn Roll, the 1890 Roll and the 1895 Roll. At that time on the much earlier Dunn Roll her name was listed as Minnie Grayson.[23]

On the reverse side of the card, the names of her parents are found. Her father was Daniel Grayson, and her mother's name was Sallie Grayson. Her father Daniel was also Creek, and a member of North Fork Town. He had at one time been enslaved by Robert Grayson. Her mother Sallie, though deceased at the time, was said to have been a Chickasaw Freedman.

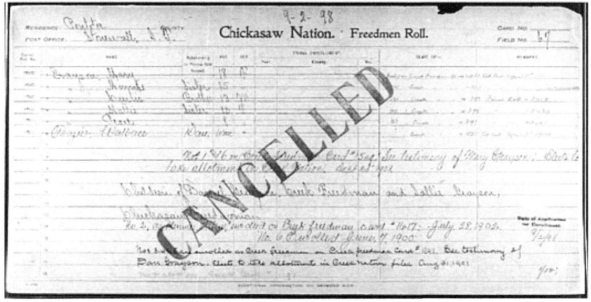

Back of Creek Enrollment Card #1461, Field Card #1617.

Parents and Siblings

Because of the Chickasaw status of Minnie's mother, Sallie, there was need to look for a possible tie to Chickasaw Freedmen. In addition, because Minnie resided in Stonewall, clearly, we needed to look further because Stonewall had a sizeable Chickasaw Freedmen population. Surprisingly, Minnie's family was located on a "cancelled" Chickasaw Freedmen card.

Front of Cancelled Chickasaw Enrollment Card #67 of Mary Grayson's family.

---

[23] Creek Enrollment Card #1461, Field Card #1617, in *Records of the Bureau of Indian Affairs*, Record Group 75. The National Archives at Ft. Worth, Ft. Worth, Texas 1868-1914. NAI Number: 251747.

The cancelled card reflected Minnie and all her siblings—Minnie herself was there, as were Mary Grayson, Curtis Grayson, Hattie Grayson, Pearl Grayson, and Mary's six-month-old child, Wallace Frazier. All were on Cancelled Chickasaw Freedman Field Card, #67. In addition to the family names, numerous notations are found on the card, confirming that they were in fact a Creek Family. This was the reason for cancelling the card. Each name on the this cancelled card had a line drawn through it, striking the name of the applicants from the rolls of Chickasaws, with a clear notation that this particular family residing in the town of Stonewall was not Chickasaw, but Creek.

On the back side of the card, it is clear that all were children of Daniel and Sallie Grayson. The back of this card reveals that Sallie Grayson had also been enslaved at one time by Winchester Colbert.

Back of Cancelled Chickasaw Enrollment Card #67 of Mary Grayson's family.

One small note on the bottom of the front side of the cancelled card shown above, was also revealing, for it noted that there was a testimony made by Daniel Grayson.

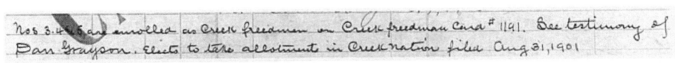

Close-up of Front of Cancelled Chickasaw Enrollment Card #67 of Mary Grayson's family.

Front of Creek Enrollment Card #873, Field Card #893.

That notation suggested that Daniel Grayson, the father, was still living. And by looking again at the Creek cards, sure enough, the children listed with Minnie on the cancelled Chickasaw card, Hattie, Curtis, and Pearl, were also found on the new Creek Freedman card, listed with their father Daniel, on Creek Enrollment Card #873, Field Card #893.

Another generation found

On the back side of Daniel Grayson's card, were the names of his parents. March Grayson and Rachel Grayson, of North Fork Town. It was noted that Rachel's name had also appeared on the Dunn Roll.

Back of Creek Enrollment Card #873, Field Card #893.

Again, noting that Rachel was not said to have been deceased, it was essential to examine the Creek Freedmen cards again. There we find an elderly woman of seventy-five years of age named Rachel. Rachel was living in the Brush Hill community which is near Checotah. And she was enrolled on Creek Freedman card #831, Field #851. Listed with her were grandchildren and a great-granddaughter.

Front of Creek Enrollment Card #831, Field #851.

Rachel was a member of North Fork Town. Her slaveholder was at one time, Jno (John) Hogeneat [?]. The mother of the children was Lizzie Grayson from North Fork Town, and Lizzie had once been enslaved by Robert Grayson, the same person who had enslaved others in this particular Grayson line.

This particular case is a good example of how essential it is to pay attention to the small notations on both sides of the card. Her card is rich with detail. In this case, noting that Rachel was still living, further examination led to her history and background. Cards such as Rachel Grayson's are uniquely valuable because she was an old woman at the time of enrollment, placing her in "the old country" before removal.

On the reverse side of the card, the names of Rachel's parents are revealed. She provides the names of both her parents—her father, Jerry, who died before the Civil War, and her mother, Angeline, who died in Mississippi. This kind of information is to be treasured by Freedmen descendants, because from this we can glean the name of the family even before the time of removal. Also if Rachel was about seventy-five years of age in 1898, when she applied for enrollment, then her birth was in the 1820s in Mississippi before the removal. Her parents would have been born in the first decade of the 1800s or earlier. The descendants of this Grayson family are fortunate as they have names from the early 1800s, if not late 1700s in their family line.

Front of Creek Enrollment Card #831, Field #851.

More information found

The question arose whether more could be learned about Minnie (Grayson) Allen herself. The answer was found in another record. In the Land Allotment jacket the "voice" of Minnie Allen can be found! She had lived for many years in the Chickasaw Nation, but her land allotment was in the Creek Nation.

She was asked about her knowledge of the Curtis Act and with which tribe specifically was she electing to enroll and receive land allotment. She clearly stated that she was electing to be enrolled as a citizen from the Creek Nation.

DEPARTMENT OF THE INTERIOR
COMMISSION TO THE FIVE CIVILIZED TRIBES
MUSKOGEE, I. T., JULY 25, 1902

In the matter of the application of Minnie Allen for the enrollment of herself as a citizen of the Creek Nation

* * *

Minnie Allen being first duly sworn, testified as follows:

(By the Commission)

Q. What is your name? A. Minnie Allen.
Q. What is your age? A. About 21
Q. What is your post office address? A. Stonewall, I. T.
Q. Are you a citizen of the Creek Nation? A. Yes.
Q. Have you ever been listed for enrollment by the Commission to the Five Civilized Tribes as a citizen of the Creek Nation? A. I have not.

(By the Commission)
The records of the Commission show that Minnie Grayson is listed for enrollment as a citizen of the Creek Nation on Creek Freedmen Field No. 581.

Q. Are you married? A. Yes, sir.
Q. What is the name of your husband? A. Thomas Allen.
Q. What was your name before you were married? A. Minnie Grayson.
Q. What is the name of your father? A. Daniel Grayson.
Q. Is he a citizen of the Creek Nation? A. Yes, sir.

(By the Commission)
The records of the Commission show that Daniel Grayson is regularly listed for enrollment as a citizen of the Creek Nation, Creek Freedman Card 893.
Q. What is the name of your mother? A. Sallie Grayson.
Q. Is she a citizen of the Creek Nation? A. No, sir.
Q. Of what nation is she a citizen? A. Chickasaw.
Q. Did you ever make application to the Commission for the enrollment of yourself as a citizen of the Chickasaw Nation? A. No, sir.
Q. Did anyone make application for you? A. Not as I know of.

(By the Commission)
The records of the Commission show that Minnie Grayson is listed for enrollment as a citizen of the Chickasaw Nation, on Chickasaw Freedman Card No. 67.
Q. Does your name appear on the tribal rolls of the Creek Nation   A. I don't know.

(By the Commission)
The authenticated 1890 roll of North Fork Town examined, and the name of Minnie Grayson is found thereon at page 153. The 1895 pay-roll of North Fork town examined and the name Minnie Grayson found theron at No. 422.

Q. Have you ever lived in the Creek Nation? A. No, sir.

(By the Commission)
Q. Are you advised that the act of June 28, 1898 known as the Curtis act provides "that several tribes may by agreement determine the right who, for any reason may claim citizenship and the distribution of moneys belonging to each tribe; but if no such agreement be made, then such claimant shall be entitled to such rights in one tribe only, and may elect in which Nation he shall take such rights."

Now, in what nation do you elect to be enrolled and receive this allotment of land and moneys? A. Creek Nation.

Edward B. Miller, being duly sworn on oath states that as stenographer to the Commission to the Five Civilized Tribes he reported in full the proceedings had in above entitled cause, on the 25th day of July 1902, and that the foregoing is a full, true, correct and complete transcript of his stenographic notes of said proceedings of said day.

Ed. B. Miller

Sworn and subcribed to before me at Muskogee, I. T. this 25th day of July 1902.
— W.S. Birell[24]

There are other items in the file with evidence that Minnie and the others did get to select their allotments as Creek citizens. From a simple file reflecting a young woman, we found the history of a family going back multiple generations. Hopefully some remnants of their legacy remain upon the soil of the Creek Nation where their history is strongly rooted.

---

[24] Ancestry.com. *Oklahoma and Indian Territory, Land Allotment Jackets for Five Civilized Tribes, 1884-1934* [database on-line]. Provo, UT, USA: Ancestry.com Operations, Inc, 2014.

Monday Barnett and Family of the Creek Nation

The Barnett family has strong roots in the Creek Nation. This family has a rich history going back to the days before the Civil War. Monday Barnett was forty-nine years of age when he appeared in front of the Dawes Commission to apply for enrollment of himself, his son Alfred, and his daughter Leoda. They actually resided in Tullahassee, and they were all members of Arkansas Town. At one time, Monday was enslaved by Dick Barnett in the Creek Nation.

Front of Creek Enrollment Card #956, Field Card #978.

Monday's father was Ketch Barnett, and his mother was Katie. Dick Barnett was the slaveholder of Ketch, and Katie had been enslaved by Katie Nicole. All the family members were members of Arkansas

Town. Although Monday's parents were deceased by the time of the Dawes Commission, they were enumerated on the Dunn Roll many years earlier.

Back of Creek Enrollment Card #956, Field Card #978.

Although no Application jacket exists for this Barnett family, another glimpse at the family's history comes through son Alfred's interview in the 1930s with the Indian Pioneer Project. What is fascinating is that he also provides a brief sketch about the life of his grandfather Ketch Barnett, who was a leader during his time. Ketch Barnett traveled with a delegation of Creeks to Washington to speak on behalf of Creek Freedmen. His associates were Harry Island and Cow Tom. Alfred Barnett was interviewed on May 24, 1937.

Interview with Alfred Barnett

I was born October 10 1875 near the old Fountain Church, in the McIntosh settlement, Creek Nation.

My father was Monday Barnett, son of Ketch Barnett.

My mother was Mandy (Marshall) Barnett (Part Creek) the daughter of John and Louisa Marshall.

I was reared and spent my past life in the immediate vicinity of my birth place. My first schooling was in the old Fountain Baptist Church which was a log structure then located on high ground just west of the McIntosh or Jamison cemetery. I was always informed by my parents and grandparents that Fountain Baptist Church was the first church organized and the old log structure the first church built in the Indian Territory. In later years when the condition of the old log church would not permit its further use, there was another church building constructed three miles west and one mile south of the original location.

In 1901, I was married to Pinkey Morey. Nine children were born to us, which are all living at the time of this writing.

* * *

KETCH BARNETT

Ketch Barnett, my grandfather, was a Baptist minister. For many years he was pastor of the old Fountain Church. He was also active in the administrative affairs of the Creek Nation in the interest of the freedmen.

After the civil war and the freedmen were granted their citizenship in the Creek Nation the Creek Indians refused to recognize the rights of the freedmen. Ketch Barnett, with Harry Island and Cow Tom went to Washington DC as a representative committee of freedmen from three districts in the Creek Nation. They pleaded the cause of the freedmen before the secretary of the interior, and the fruit of the mission was the making of the "Dunn" Creek roll and the freedmen having equal rights in tribal payments and allotments with the full blood Creeks.

I do not know when Ketch Barnett was born, but he came to the Indian Territory, in 1832 with Ben Marshall as one of Ben Marshall's slaves. He died in 1875.

According to Albert's interview, Ketch Barnett was also a Baptist minister and was pastor of Fountain Baptist church. The only difference is that he refers to a different person as the slaveholder of his grandfather, and says that his grandfather was enslaved by Ben Marshall.

Fountain Church was a major church on its own in the mid to late 1800s. In one of the Pioneer interviews, a sketch was actually made of the original church, where Monday's father Ketch Barnett was pastor. The sketch is found in the interview with Charles W. Ponds, of Muskogee conducted in April 1937. And also thanks to the interview with grandson Alfred, we know the actual death date of Ketch Barnett.[25]

Sketch found in Indian Pioneer Project interview with Charles W. Ponds.

---

[25] Ibid.

Land Allotment Records

Thankfully the land records do exist for the Barnett family, and through the words of Alfred we also find more about his father, Monday Barnett. In 1900, Monday appeared in front of the commission, and he spoke on behalf of himself regarding his land in the Wybark area.

DEPARTMENT OF THE INTERIOR
COMMISSION TO THE FIVE CIVILIZED TRIBES
MUSCOGEE, I. T., JAN. 12TH 1900

IN THE MATTER OF THE APPLICATION OF MONDAY BARNETT, for allotment as a citizen of the Muscogee Nation, accompanied by a proper description of the land applied for and a certificate that he is entitled to take in accordance with the rules of the Secretary of the Interior, and he being sworn by Commissioner, T. B. Needles, testified as follows:

Q. What is your name? A. Monday Barnett.

Q. Are you a citizen of the Muscogee Nation? A. Yes, sir.

Q. What town do you belong to? A. Arkansas

Q. Is your name on the Dunn Roll? A. Yes, sir.

Q. How long have you lived in the Creek Nation? A. All my life.

Q. Have you been outside of the Indian Territory in the last two years? A. No sir.

Q. What is your post office address? A. Wybark, I. T.

Q. Do you own a home of your own in the Creek Nation? A. Yes, sir.

Q. Is this your home place you are now filing on? A. Yes, sir.

Q. Are you in possession of it? A. Yes, sir.

Q. You make application for yourself for the west half of the north west quarter of the south west quarter of the north east quarter., the east half of the north east quarter of the south west quarter, and the north half of the north west quarter of the south east quarter of section 28 township 16, range 18, is that correct? A. Yes, sir.

Q. Who lives in the house? A. I do.

Q. How many acres under cultivation on that land? A. About twenty acres.

Q. Is the improved land fenced? A. Yes, sir.

Q. Does anyone else claim this land or any part of it? A. No, sir.

Q. Do you know where this land is? A. Yes, sir.

Q. Have you seen it and been over it? A. Yes, sir.

Q. Have you examined it, intending to make this application for it? A. Yes, sir.

Q. Is it prairie land or timber land? A. Timber land.

Q. Is this land suitable for a home for yourself? A. Yes, sir.

Q. Are you making this application in good faith in all respects? A. Yes, sir.

Q. Will you accept this land as part of your final allotment? A. Yes, sir.

Q. Are there any churches, schoolhouses, or burial grounds on this land? A. No, sir.

WITNESS:

R. R. Cravens

Monday Barnett his (X) mark

[Illegible]

Sworn to and subscribed to before me this 12 day of Jan. 1900 at Muscogee, I. T.

[Illegible]

A year later, we later see in 1901 where Alfred represents his father with Power of Attorney. It is not clear if Monday was gravely ill or not. The land that was being allotted was partly timberland, and not farm land or prairie land.

We do not know when Monday Barnett passed, but the Barnett family history is a rich one. On the one enrollment card, multiple generations are illustrated. This family with ties to Creek Freedmen leader Ketch Barnett has a colorful history and past. Their history predates removal. Hopefully the Creek legacy is honored and respected by descendants to this day.

Julia Hershey and Family

Researching families from the Creek Nation is not without its difficulties. This is particularly when one finds that so many of the interviews of families are simply missing. They were misplaced, and never microfilmed and now lost to time. Therefore when one finds some remarkable stories in the application jackets that were preserved they should be shared as they provide so many insights into the lives of people in the nineteenth century in Indian Territory. Such is the case of Julia Hershey (Hersche) from Muskogee. She appeared in front of the Dawes Commission in September 1898.

She was fifty-four years of age when she applied for enrollment as a Creek Freedman. On Field Card #1222 her name is found with that of her son John Pyles, who was eighteen. She was a member of Arkansas Town and had been enslaved by Lookin Barnett. Some notations on the front of the card indicate that she had been placed on earlier rolls over many years.[26]

Front of Creek Enrollment Card #1143, Field #1222.

[26] Creek Enrollment Card #1143, Field Card #1222, in *Records of the Bureau of Indian Affairs*, Record Group 75. The National Archives at Ft. Worth, Ft. Worth Texas 1868-1914 NAI Number: 251747.

On the reverse side of the card the names of her parents are found. Her father was Alex Barnett and her mother was Rosa Barnett who had died during the years of the Civil War. Lish Pyles was her son's father, and he was not a citizen of the Creek Nation.

Back of Creek Enrollment Card #1143, Field #1222.

The Application Jacket

To say that the data contained in her application jacket was plentiful does not say enough. There are thirty-three pages contained in the file. Many of the questions asked of Julia go far beyond the ordinary questions that one typically sees in the application jackets. Of course the usual personal data about her life was there, but in addition, one can read about the detailed application process that people went through to prove who they were. One can glean from this file the numerous people that she met in her life, and the various relationships she had with people are detailed. It is also clear that like many others, Freedmen had formed relationships and friendships with those from other tribes in addition to the tribe in which they lived.

Personal Data About the Applicant

There are multiple interviews in the file, and most of them occurred in 1899. Julia first appeared in front of the commission in May of 1899. Then later in September, she appeared again. In November of that year, Nannie Murray, a Cherokee citizen appeared on her behalf, and then in December, Willie McIntosh spoke on her behalf.

DEPARTMENT OF THE INTERIOR
COMMISSION TO THE FIVE CIIVLIZED TRIBES
Muskogee Land Office, Tuesday, May 2nd, 1899

In the matter of the application of Julia Hersche.

JULIA HERSCHE, being sworn and examined, testified as follows:

Q. How old are you Julia? About how old? A. This August coming I will be about 54 years old.
Q. What was your father's name? A. Alex Barnett
Q. Was he a citizen of any Indian tribe? A. (no response recorded)
A. Lareken Burnett (question not recorded)

Q. Then he was a Creek Freedman? A. Yes, sir.

Q. What was your mother's name? A. Rose Barnett.

Q. Did she belong to any Creek Indian? A. She belonged to some folks; belonged to Granny Black; she was an Indian.

Q. Creek Indian? A. I guess it was, her old was an Indian.

Q. Is your father living? A. No sir.

Q. Is your mother? A. No sir.

Q. When did your mother die? A. I don't know how long.

Q. Was it before or after peace? A. Before peace.

Q. Where were you living at the time peace was declared? A. Fannin County Texas.

Q. Who had you belonged to before that time? A. Grannie Black.

Q. How did you get down into Texas? A. They went out there with the Indians, drove out there.

Q. They carried you out there to Texas? A. Yes, sir.

Q. You were there when they told you that peace was declared and set you free. You were living in Fannin County Texas when they told you that peace had been declared and that you were free? A. Yes sir.

Q. What did you do or where did you go? A. After peace was delivered, I came back here.

Q. How soon? A. I came back the next year when they said the treaty of 1866, the Indians was to come back and get here in time, for the treaty of 1866 and I came back with a whole lot of Indians.

Q. What Indians did you come with? A. I can't tell.

Q. Did you have any relatives in the crowd? A. No sir, the Indians I came with didn't have no clothes on. They had these little diapers or britch cloths and part of them came in go-carts what have jacks and jennies. I came with them to Gibson, and stopped there a while, and they all disappeared, first one place and another, and I stayed there a while and came across over here and went out to the Old Agency and stayed there a while after that.

Q. Who did you stay with at the Old Agency? Who did you live with? A. I don't know. I can't call that woman's name; she was an old bronze-skinned woman.

Q. Indian or colored woman? A. Colored woman, like Aunt Fishe, I can't remember her name. She was an old woman, pretty near like Iska Durant

Q. When you came back to Fort Gibson, did you hear the Indians and colored people talk about going up to the Old Agency to give in their names? A. Yes, sir, I went over there with some of them and I don't know what they meant by putting people down on the roll, and stayed there when the men went out and came again I didn't know what they was doing and they wanted something to pay them, and we didn't have none.

Q. Who asked you? A. That man putting them on the roll, Dunn something.

Q. You say Mr. Dunn asked you to pay him before putting your name on the roll? A. I didn't have no money to pay nothing.

Q. You looked after your own business? A. I came home to get with my people, Dick Barnett.

Q. Was he your uncle? A. Yes, sir, own dear uncle.

Q. Is he living now? A. Uncle Bob, died. I can't tell how long its been.

Q. Have you got any other besides Dick? A. Uncle's wife, she is living and married Wm. Perryman.

Q. What's her name? A. Nancy—I don't forgot her name, I didn't see her even.

Q. How long did you stay up around the old Agency with that old woman you lived with? A. I reckon I stayed near about a month, backward and forward. I would go backward and forward first to Gibson and then over there.

Q. Do you remember when they began to pay out money at Old Agency? A. I didn't get it.

Q. Do you remember the time they paid it out? A. Yes, sir.

Q. Did you ever ask for any money? A. No sir, I just stayed around and looked at the rest get it and they didn't give me any and I never asked for it.

Q. They never called your name? A. No, sir.

Q. How long did you stay at the Old Agency back and forth between there and Ft. Gibson? A. I don't know how long I stayed, it has been so long.

Q. When did you go down to Ft. Smith to live? A. I can't tell you how many years it has been. I wasn't living there all the time. I would go hire out and make money and come back here. We was also at Temple and worked there a while and come back up here and stayed around.

Q. That's the way you missed getting the $29.00? A. I reckon. I was at the Old Agency when they were giving all the money.

Q. That was the Dunn payment? A. I suppose.

Q. That was about $17.00 was it? A. I don't know.

Q. Do you remember about ten years ago when they all drew $29.00? A. Yes sir, I remember that.

Q. You didn't get $29.00? A. No sir, I didn't get $29.00.

Q. Do you know where they were when they paid out the $29.00? A. They were at the Old Agency.

Q. You are sure you wasn't living at Ft. Smith? A. No, sir.

Q. Are you sure this was paid at the Old Agency? You don't know what the $29.00 payment is? A. I was there when they were paying money.

Q. Do you remember the time when Judge Moore paid out any money. A. Judge Moore paid out some money in the bank.

Q. How much a head? A. Bread money, he called it. I was there, and when they came to my name, they got to Julia Barnett, it was tore off. Just as they called my name I was sitting like I am now, and they told me I would have to get up and step aside.

Q. Did you ever draw money from the Creeks? A. Yes, sir.

Q. How much was it? A. Fourteen dollars and something.

Q. Who did you draw for? A. Myself and boy.

Q. What was his name? A. Jim Pyles.

Q. That's the only time you ever drew money? A. Yes, sir. I guess I would have drawed it if this hadn't been—they told me if I wanted any money I couldn't have it, but if I wanted land I could go and take up all the land I wanted.

Q. When was that told you? A. At Okmulgee twice.

Q. Do you know who told you that? A. Buz Hawkins.

Q. Buz Hawkins knew you? A. I don't know sir, I reckon he did.

Q. Had you then been acquainted with Buz Hawkins some time before that? A. I knowed him, but never was acquainted much, but knowed him whenever I seen him.

Q. How long before you drew the fourteen dollars was it you came back from Fort Smith? A. I don't know.

Q. How many times have you been married? A. Twice.

Q. What was your first husband's name? A. Pyles.

Q. What was his full name? A. Lish Pyles.

Q. He was Jim's father? A. Yes, sir.

Q. Then you were afterwards married to a man called Harsha? A. William Harsha.

Q. Was Lish Pyles or William Hersha citizens? A. No, sir.

Q. Were they State men? A. Yes, sir.

Julia's interview goes on for many more pages. Several people appeared on her behalf. Tobe McIntosh was examined and many questions were asked about their movements during and after the war, pertaining to their time in Texas, the location where they lived, and questions about the time after the war, returning to Ft. Gibson. Several months later more interviews were conducted. Needless to say, this file is worth examining in its entirety, because the story emerges of how those once enslaved fared in those early days of freedom. Their movement from one encampment to another, and the treatment of the former slaves during the periods of per capita payments and having names places on official records such as the Dunn Roll are revealed.

Another interesting witness on her behalf was a Cherokee woman whose name was Nannie Murray. Nannie Murray was asked about her knowledge of Julia and the family and she pointed out that she knew that Julia's mother was enslaved by Granny Black. (The reference to Granny Black also appears in the first interview above.) She was then asked to confirm the relationship of Julia to Granny Black the slaveholder. Nannie pointed out that she never was at the home of Granny Black, but her own grandmother used to visit Granny Black, and Granny Black used to visit them. She learned from those visits in her childhood that Granny Black owned her mother "Rhody" and that Rhody had three children.

Again there were questions about the tie of Julia to the Blacks, and Nannie confirmed that Granny Black (the Creek Indian woman) used to make references to "her colored folks" frequently. She was then asked if she knew Charlotte Blackdirt, which she said at first she did not know. But then she replied that she knew that Charlotte had married a Lewis, but was not sure if Granny Black had owned Charlotte. When asked why she referred to her as "Aunt Charlotte" she pointed out that many people of color referred to other in that way.

To summarize the many interviews in this file, it is worth reading because these depositions reflect the complexity of the relationships that existed between the enslaved and the slaveholders, and the nature of their relationships after freedom came.

Tribal Town Officials Testify for Julia

One of the more interesting documents in the Julia Hersche file comes from an official of Arkansas Colored Town. It should be pointed out that the tribal town system in the Creek Nation was one of the more unique systems, where there were "towns" but not in a residential sense. There were political "districts" to which people belonged. One's name was put on a "town" roll which reflected their affiliation with the tribe through their town. Each town had a representative in the two ruling houses of the nation—the House of Warriors and the House of Kings. The town therefore had a "Warrior" and a "King" representing them when the tribal council met.

One of the witnesses for Julia was Willie McIntosh, who had an official role in his town as Secretary for the Arkansas Colored Town. He was present when citizens came to draw the various payments over the years and verified that he knew her. He was also asked if he knew a Julia who was part of the Derishaw family, which he did not. He verified that he knew that Julia drew the money and was asked more than one time how he was certain of it. He was then presented with a document and asked if it was in his handwriting. He pointed out that it was not done by his hand, but it was copied from his own book. There then seemed to be satisfaction enough that Julia was qualified for enrollment.

A year later, Julia appeared again in front of the commission. She was asked about her parents. Alex Barnett was enslaved by Larkin (Lookin) Barnet, and her mother was enslaved by Granny Black. Her mother died before the war ended, although it was not mentioned where.

For the researcher, one can see the movement of people across the countryside, some to Fort Gibson, and others to other settlements in Indian Territory. Some were in search of family and others in search of a way to make their life. Julia described how she had moved from Fort Gibson to Muskogee, and she pointed out how many times she appeared for payments to Creeks. She also described having her name put on the Dunn Roll. Following that were multiple pages about her receiving various payments over the years. Various payments from "Bread money" and other payments made over the years. She was grilled continuously about who distributed the funds to her and where. Then witnesses were called to verify that she was truly the same Julia. These questions continued for numerous pages in the file.

The Town King's Testimony

One of the more fascinating interviews in Julia's file came from Gabriel Jamison. He was the town king for Arkansas Colored Town. The line of questioning was focused on Julia's name on the Arkansas Colored Town roll. When asked if her name was there and how it was done, he decided to describe the entire process of creating the town roll. His description provides a clear insight into exactly how things happened from inside the Creek political structure, and also structure the of the tribal towns. See the excerpt that follows from the testimony of Gabriel Jamison.[27]

Testimony of Gabriel Jamison

Q. When you first got the rolls was Julia's name on the Arkansas roll?

A. I am going to tell that part. When I got to be town king we had a spite, we had a row in the Nation and that's after I got to be town king. I could'nt get hold of the Arkansas roll. All the rolls were scattered. The Canadian, Arkansas, and North Fork, and in the time of making application we reported to the Chief and he turned around and gave orders to get up the roll and enroll the people. We turned around and enrolled up here. Buz Hawkins and old man Scipio Sango and others and the people came in and so we got ready and took it to Omulgee; three town kings took up that. That's the time old man Scipio Sango gave me my name, King of Canadian Town. After we got to Okmulgee they turned around and appointed an 18 committee to examine the rolls and every town king to be present, then they had the colored people to prove who was on that and they went on until they got the roll completed and after we got through, a good many was thrown off; they could'nt give account of who they was and they left them out. Every person who was left on the roll some other person would identify them. After we got through with the roll before the 18 committee, it went before the house and was adopted.

Q. Was she on that roll and identified? A. Yes sir.

Q. Who identified her? Scipio Sango, town king of the Canadian Town. A. No sir, he is dead.

Q. Do you know what year it was that the 18 committee made up that roll? A. It must be 16. I served about 12 years and I have been out going on four years now. That was the first year I went in. I went in the next coming fall was the year they got them up.

Q. You never heard of her being on the Arkansas roll before that time? A. Was'nt on before that time.

Many pages following that were devoted to why Julia's name was left off several rolls from the $29 payment roll to the "Omitted" Roll. For those whose ancestors went through this process, it will be worthwhile to explore each and every page of this lengthy file.

Oddly, as detailed as the file was, the ending to the case was abrupt. Julia was recalled again, and was asked about the exact age of her son, and why some data conflicted with other data. She pointed out that at times her mind would come and go and she was not sure. She was then directed to present any additional testimony on June 12th for her next interview. And thus the file ended.

---

[27] *Applications for Enrollment of the Commission to the Five Civilized Tribes, 1898–1914.* Microfilm M1301, 468 rolls. NAI: 617283. Records of the Bureau of Indian Affairs, Record Group 75. The National Archives at Washington, D.C.

But it should be noted that the abrupt ending of the file does not diminish the file, nor the case. In fact the rich data contained on those pages far outweighs the seemingly abrupt ending. Julia Hershey was clearly a woman of the Creek Nation and clearly her case was eventually approved and not rejected. She left behind an amazing narrative describing her life from the end of the war, her travels back to Fort Gibson, and her life over the years. As the nation changed, her status changed, and she was a witness to the many changes within Indian Territory.

She got her land as did her son. This Creek woman, whose education was limited, survived nevertheless. From her file, we see part of her life described before emancipation. We see the early days of freedom as her life dramatically changed. We also see the years spent in different places, as different circumstances required movement sometimes for work and other times to find better living situations. Her relationship with the tribe is apparent, and the relationship that former slaves had to the land and the community was strong. From this one woman's files, so much is learned. May her Creek descendants come to read, embrace, and grow from her story.[28]

---

[28] The entire file of Julia Hershey can be found in Application Jacket #1222, in microfilm collection M1301 at the National Archives. It can also be accessed online at Ancestry.com.

Part 2. Seminole Freedmen

Seminole Freedmen—An Introduction

The unique history of Seminole Freedmen has a multi-state origin. In the early nineteenth century, as many enslaved people sought freedom, they fled southward to Florida from the Carolinas and Georgia, seeking freedom. Once there, they found themselves among another community of people who had fled Alabama. Red Stick warriors, a group once part of the Creeks of Alabama, soon found themselves allied with the freedom seekers. They all found themselves needing to share resources to fight a common enemy. The former slaves resisted slave catchers and fought to remain free in the maroon communities of Florida. The natives had broken away from the Creeks in their native Alabama and Georgia and for many years were able to resist military efforts to subdue them. During the Seminole Wars, the U.S. military fought both to capture runaway slaves, and also to quell conflicts with natives, and the freedmen and the natives became allies.

Among African leaders who engaged in the conflicts were leaders such as Kojo, Abraham, Ben Bruner, and others who would serve in numerous roles over the years. It is also important to note that in the years before removal to the west there was much conflict with federal authorities when the U.S. government made efforts to relocate the Seminoles to the Indian Territory without the blacks, but the Seminoles resisted as they did not wish to relocate without the Africans who had become their compatriots.

Finally, after much conflict, the two groups—Africans and Seminoles—were relocated to Indian Territory after the Second Seminole War, and once in the Territory, they lived near each other for decades. But Seminoles have a particularly distinct history. Although many of the Africans among them had been enslaved in the Carolinas and Georgia, there were also many among them who were free people and had never been enslaved. It is said by some writers that the slavery practiced in Seminole country was distinct and might be viewed by some as a "less harsh" form of enslavement. But the institution of slavery *did* exist and was still practiced by some native groups including some of the Seminole leaders who arrived in the Territory.

In the post-Civil War years, those once enslaved, and their children, were identified as "Freedmen." But in addition, even those who were born free in Florida, and who had never been enslaved, also ended up being referred to as "Freedmen."

Despite the classification, there was still movement socially between the two different classes of people. African Seminoles still had an alliance with those who had fled Alabama during the Red Stick conflicts, and Seminole natives maintained an alliance with others who had fled the Carolinas seeking freedom. Freedmen became an integral part of the Seminole Nation. Many served on the tribal council, others as interpreters, and others as leaders of their respective bands of Seminole citizens.

The works of two scholars—Dr. Daniel F. Littlefield, and Dr. Kevin Mulroy, have explored this unique history in depth, and it is imperative that any student of Seminole Freedmen history study their works. Both authors go into detail about the structure of the communities, and how the Seminole Freedmen and the bands evolved. Those Africans belonged to clans or bands that preceded the present-day Barkus and Bruner bands were known as the Jim Lane Band, the John Brown Band, and the Pompey Payne Band. Today two bands remain from the smaller bands of the late nineteenth century—the Dosar Barkus band and the Caesar Bruner band.

Education in the early years was undertaken in some Seminole schools such as Mikasukey, but after separation was ordered in the Territory, some freedmen obtained education at the Creek Seminole College for Freedmen, in Boley. In addition to social interaction there was much contact on other levels. Trade was cordial between the Freedmen and Seminole communities. There was also intermarriage between Seminole Freedmen and Creek Freedmen. It turns out that two leaders of the Freedmen, one Creek and one Seminole, were in fact full brothers—Caesar Bruner, Seminole, was a full brother to Paro Bruner, Creek—and their stories are outlined in this volume.

When it came to the time of the Dawes allotment era, Seminoles had no objection to Freedmen being treated equally during the process. Scholar Kevin Mulroy pointed out in his book on Seminole Freedmen that there were *"no discretionary clauses regarding the rights of the freedmen."* And we note that the process of enrollment in the Seminole Nation was a smooth one.

However, the challenge for the researcher today, is the fact that there are numerous missing files for Seminoles. This includes Seminoles "By Blood" as well as Seminole "Freedmen." For the purpose of research, we must rely on collections beyond the Dawes records to document the stories of Seminole Freedmen. Thankfully, land allotment records as well as interviews from the Indian Pioneer Papers, assist in this process.

It should be noted that many resources were used to find data on these families. In some cases a name was spelled one way on the Dawes cards, and years later during the Pioneer Interviews from the 1930s, the spelling was different. This is noted in the cases of the surname Fulsom, sometimes written as Folsom. This was also the case where the name Myers was written years later as Meyers, and Paro was written as Perry. Extensive research was done to insure that there were not two distinct people, with similar names, and that in both cases they were the same person.

The effort to document these Seminole Freedmen families will be useful for the researcher of Seminole history. Though research challenges still face members of both Barkus and Bruner bands today, they stand on a unique and rich legacy. As their struggle to remain a full part of their nation continues, we find motivation in the words that described their status as Seminoles.

"As long as the grass grows and the rivers flow, we shall be one."

We hope that their legacy will prevail. This portion of volume 2 supports the amazingly rich history of the Seminole Freedmen.

The Family of Becca James Carter

Becca Carter was the mother of several children. She appeared in front of the Dawes Commission to enroll herself and her children as members of the Barkus band in the Seminole Nation. which has always been structured by bands. With this particular family, it is clear that they are part of the Dosar Barkus band. That band was and still is one of the two freedmen bands in the Seminole Nation today.

The entry on the enrollment card points out that Becca's husband was a Creek citizen, explaining why his name is not on the front of this enrollment card. It also notes that one of her daughters—Rachel—later married by the time the rolls were finalized and became the wife of Nero Noble. He was a Seminole and was placed on the rolls by blood while her children were placed on a Freedman New Born card.[29]

Front of Seminole Enrollment Card No. 623, of Becca Carter and Family.

---

[29] *Enrollment Cards for the Five Civilized Tribes, 1898-1914;* NAI Number: 251747. *Records of the Bureau of Indian Affairs;* Record Group Number 75. The National Archives at Ft Worth; Ft Worth, Texas, USA.

Becca was forty-five years old at the time the card was completed and thus was born before slavery had ended in Indian Territory. Therefore information on the slaveholder is provided on the card. She was once enslaved by Eliza Bowlegs. Also note that there is no date on the enrollment card, but it is obvious that she appeared in front of the Commission after 1897, because the card notes that she and her family had previously been enrolled as members of the Barkus band on the 1897 roll.

The reverse side of the card reveals more of Becca Carter's history. Her father was Cyrus Davis and her mother was Polly Carter. The slaveholder of both her parents was Eliza Bowlegs. Both her parents were also at one time members of the Dosar Barkus band. Becca's husband's name was James Carter, and he is listed as the father of the children in the household. A notation points out that he was "free born." However not much more is known of him.

Back of Seminole Enrollment Card No. 623, of Becca Carter and Family.

A quick search of the Dawes Records does not provide information on James Carter's enrollment as a Creek Freedman. Unfortunately, the Dawes Packet for Seminole Freedmen Card No. 623 is not available. A range of Dawes packets are said to simply be empty, and Becca's packet is among the empty ones. (see following image):

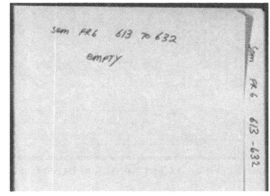

Folder Reflecting Empty Contents

So the question arose whether additional information about the family could be found. Clues to additional family data were found on the front of the card itself. A notation appears stating that Becca and her family were previously enrolled in 1897.

Close-up of Front of Seminole Enrollment Card No. 623.

On Ancestry.com there is an extensive collection of records from Oklahoma and Indian Territory, beyond the Dawes Rolls. One of those extensive collections is called *Indian Censuses and Rolls 1851-1959.* This covers a period of more than a century, and it includes records from the Five Civilized Tribes. Within that collection there is a section of documents reflecting the 1897 Seminole Census. Sure enough Becca—called "Becky"—was on that roll with her children.[30]

The document came from a small collection from Fort Worth Texas with earlier records from the Seminole Nation. Thanks to a partnership with the National Archives, and also with the Oklahoma Historical Society, that 1895 Seminole census document is now available. This microfilm collection published by the National Archives in Fort Worth, and is found under the microfilm collection, 7RA-287, Bureau of Indian Affairs.

This collection also contains other Seminole Rolls, including the 1867 Seminole Payment Roll, the 1895-1896 Seminole Roll, the 1897 Seminole Roll, the 1900 Seminole Miscellaneous Roll, the 1901 Seminole $14 Roll. They were all microfilmed in 1992 at the National Archives in Ft. Worth. Since this set of records did contain, the 1897 Seminole Roll, Becca and her family were indeed found on the 1897 census Roll as well. (See following image.)

---

[30] Ancestry.com. *Oklahoma and Indian Territory, Indian Censuses and Rolls, 1851-1959* [database on-line]. Provo, UT, USA: Ancestry.com Operations, Inc., 2014. Original data: *Selected Tribal Records.* The National Archives at Fort Worth, Fort Worth, Texas. . (The page is reflecting image number 60 of 467 images in this collection on Ancestry.)

Pages 160-161 of the 1897 Seminole Roll.[31]

Close-up of Front of Seminole Enrollment Card No. 623, of Becca Carter and Family.

[31] Ancestry.com. *Oklahoma and Indian Territory, Indian Censuses and Rolls, 1851-1959* [database on-line]. Provo, UT, USA: Ancestry.com Operations, Inc., 2014. Original data: *Selected Tribal Records*. The National Archives at Fort Worth, Fort Worth, Texas. (The page is image number 107 of 467 images in this collection on Ancestry.com.)

So although the Dawes packet was not available, could other things about the family be learned? The front of the census card did note that Becca's children had later become parents. On the bottom of the card were notes on where to find the children of Becca's children.[32]

The Seminole New Born collection reflected the enrollment of a grandchild of Becca Carter—that of Alec Carter. Alec was the son of Philip Carter, Becca's son. In that file was an extensive interview plus a birth record for the child.[33]

DEPARTMENT OF THE INTERIOR
COMMISSION TO THE FIVE CIVILIZED TRIBES
Wewoka, Indian Territory, May 15, 1905

In the matter of the application for the enrollment of Alec Carter as a citizen of the Seminole Nation.

George Jones being duly sworn, testified as follows through Mrs. A. B. Davis, official interpreter:

Q. What is your name? A. George Jones.

Q. How old are you? A. 29.

Q. Do you know Phillip Carter? A. Yes, sir.

Q. You are his band chief? A. Yes, sir.

Q. Did you know Sally Carter? A. Yes, sir.

Q. Is Sally Carter now living? A. No sir, she is dead.

Q. When did she die? A. She died in February, I think, in 1902.

Q. Did Sally Carter have any children? A. Yes, sir.

Q. How many? A. One.

Q. Do you know the name of that child? A. I have forgotten his name, I knew it.

Q. You would know this child if you were to see it? A. Yes, sir.

Q. Is this the child? (indicating Alec Carter). A. Yes, sir.

Q. Does the name of Alec Carter, the child of Sally Carter, appear upon your roll as a member of your band? A. Yes, sir.

Q. Has he ever drawn any headright? A. Yes, sir, he is on my roll.

Q. How long has he been on that roll; ever since he was born? A. Yes, sir.

Q. Do you know why the name of this child was not place on the former approved roll? A. I have only been band chief for a short time, and this child's name was on the band roll when I took charge.

---

[32] *Enrollment Cards for the Five Civilized Tribes, 1898-1914;* NAI Number: 251747; *Records of the Bureau of Indian Affairs;* Record Group Number: 75. National Archives Publication M1186 The National Archives at Ft Worth; Ft Worth, Texas, USA.
[33] *Application Packet Seminole Freedman 95.* National Archives Publication M1301.

James Carter being duly sworn, testified as follows:

Q. What is your name? A. James Carter.
Q. How old are you? A. About 58.
Q. What is your post office address? A. Tidmore.
Q. Are you a citizen of the Seminole Nation? A. No, sir, I am a citizen of the Creek Nation.
Q. Are you the father of Phillip Carter? A. Yes, sir.
Q. Did you know Sally Carter, the wife of your son? A. Yes, sir, I know her and her father and her mother.
Q. Do you know what month this child Alec Carter was born? A. I don't recollect, but I know he was born about the time they were pretty near closing the roll, because I have one little girl by the name of Maria Jackson on the roll, and that little girl was born after this child was born, but she got on in time to get her land, but this woman was sick and couldn't get down here to get hers.
Q. And for that reason this child wasn't placed on the roll? A. Yes sir, that is the reason she didn't get it, and that is what her band officers told me.

* * *

Frank C. Sabourin, being duly sworn states that the annexed page contains a true and complete transcript of his stenographic notes taken in said case on the 15th day of May, 1905

Frank C. Sabourin

Subscribed and sworn to me on this 16th day of May, 1905.
(Seal)
Charles E. Webster, Notary Public
My commission expires April 28 1909

Also in this file, James Carter, Becca's husband James appears and gives a testimony as well. As was indicated earlier, James was identified as a Creek citizen. Apparently Becca and James were separated, as he mentions that he had another child, Maria Jackson, whose mother was not enrolled.

Like most Dawes records the descendants of Becca Carter have a well-documented one, in spite of the fact that the enrollment packet is missing for the family. By searching the earlier census records, and also by following the clues in the New Born files, one can get a better glimpse of the family makeup, and the individuals whose stories are to be told.

Sample of one of the land allotment records.

Land Allotment Records

The Carter family did receive their land. In the Land Allotment jacket, there is another interview with the husband James Carter, and several documents reflecting the exact location of the land that each person in the household received.

The remaining pages in the file reflect the process they went through to finalize their allotment. More on the family can be gleaned from both this set of land records as well as the records reflecting the history of the father, James, who was a Creek Freedman. The Carter family, as members of the Barkus band, is a strong one with a legacy that hopefully continues strongly to this day.

The Legacy of Samuel and Betsey Mahardy:
Seminole (and Chickasaw) Identity

The family of Betsey Mahardy of the Seminole Nation presents a very complicated and complex family from Indian Territory. The story is complicated not because of size, but because of the family's personal identity of itself, as well as the official label that was placed upon them. It is also a complex story because of the many "types" of lives lived by the family and the generation that preceded them.

Theirs is a story of multiple family branches from a family in which some individuals were enslaved, and others born free, as well as a story of those who intermarried between tribes and a story of Africans who also had spouses who were Indians as well. And finally, this is a case that also includes one of identity and affiliation that will be reflected in one of the more extensive interviews that can be found.

Betsey Mahardy and her family resided in Wynnewood, Indian Territory, in the Chickasaw Nation. An application was made in 1899 in front of the Dawes Commission to enroll Betsey and her children as Seminoles. It was stated that she belonged to the Caesar Bruner Band of Seminole Freedmen. She was fifty-seven years old at the time and had once been enslaved by Seminole Sam Bruner.

Her sons were Richard Bruner, Samuel Mahardy and Lyman Mahardy. Betsey's parents were Charlie Stedham and Eliza Canard. Her father was once the slave of Sallie Stedham, and her mother was a slave of Seminole Wiley Canard.

Betsey's first husband, the father of her son Richard Bruner, was Sam Bruner, a Seminole Indian, and thus, always free. He had died during the Civil War. Her second husband was Wyatt Mahardy, the father of her other two sons. The question arose when their son requested to be transferred to that as Chickasaw by blood. That would become the focus of much discussion that will be illustrated in the application jacket and series of complicated interviews to follow.

However, Betsey Mahardy's enrollment card noted that Wyatt Mahardy was actually a Chickasaw by blood, and therefore a man who was "born free" according to the back of the card. Clearly, the reverse side of the card states that he was born free and had not been enslaved.

And, most interestingly, on the enrollment card itself, there was a clear boldly written notation on the front that explains the entire issue—Betsey Mahardy was married to a man who was not Seminole, but actually Chickasaw. But the note from the commission on the card, pointed out that though he was Chickasaw, "his father was a Negro."

Front of Seminole Enrollment Card #843.

Close-up of Front of Seminole Enrollment Card #843.

Back of Seminole Enrollment Card #843.

The Interviews

The application jackets contain one of the most complicated cases of identity, belonging, recognition, and self-identity, and several pages are included here. What appears on the surface to be a simple case in the enrollment cards took many directions as the case of Wyatt Mahardy unfolded. The outside cover of the file folder reveals the complicated nature, of the issues contained.

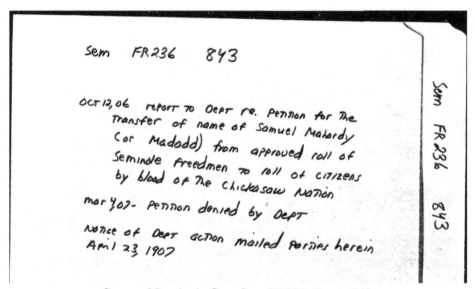

Cover of Seminole Case Sem FR236, Card #843.

Inside the file one will find several pages of letters that appear in the front of the file. The item headed by the words *"Statement of Case"* summarizes much of the multi-tribal family case. Note that the focus was placed upon the son Samuel and the request made by the father to have him removed from Seminole Freedman status to that of Chickasaw By Blood. It is worth reading in detail to glean an understanding of the complexity of the family's structure.

After many references and case numbers, then, the interview begins. Betsey Mahardy points out that she was actually Creek, thus casting doubt into data that appears about her on the enrollment card. She states that some relatives of her were the ones who had enrolled her as a Seminole Freedman, but she clearly states. *"No sir, no Seminole Indian ever owned me."*

DEPARTMENT OF THE INTERIOR
COMMISSIONER TO THE FIVE CIVILIZED TRIBES
Muskogee, Indian Territory, October 3, 1906

In the matter of the application of the transfer of the name of Samuel Mahardy (or Mahada) from the roll of Seminole freedmen to the roll of citizens by blood of the Chickasaw Nation.

STATEMENT OF CASE

The applicant Samuel Mahardy is a duly enrolled citizen of the Seminole Nation, his name appearing upon the final roll of such citizens as approved by the Secretary of the Interior on April 2, 1901 opposite No. 2740. An allotment of the lands of the Seminole Nation was arbitrarily made to the said Samuel Mahardy by the Commission to the Five Civilized Tribes on June 28, 1902.

The Commission to the Five Civilized Tribes, on November 19, 1902 refused the application of Samuel Mahardy (or Mahada) for enrollment as a citizen by blood of the Chickasaw Nation for the reason that he had been enrolled as a citizen of the Seminole Nation and had received an allotment as such. This decision of the Commission to the Five Civilized Tribes, adverse to the applicant, Samuel Mahardy, was affirmed by the Secretary of the Interior January 22, 1903. (I. T. D. 7552-1902)

She pointed out that her sister, "Ben Bruner's wife," was the relative who enrolled her, but her identity was that as being Creek, and not Seminole. The interview also goes on to inquire about her first marriage, and her marriage to Wyatt Mahardy, which was performed by John Ishtone, a well-known Seminole preacher.

Betsey Mahardy being duly sworn testifies as follows:

COMMISSIONER:

Q. What is your name? A. Betsey Mahardy.
Q. How old are you? A. I can't say just how old I am for I can't keep no account of it.
Q. Where do you live? A. In the Chickasaw Nation?
Q. What is your post office address? A. Davis
Q. Are you a citizen of the Chickasaw Nation? A. No, sir.
Q. Of what nation are you a citizen? A. I am a Creek. During the war I went out with the ones who went to the Seminole Nation, and I didn't go with the ones that came back this way.
Q. Didn't you belong to a Seminole Indian? A. No sir, no Seminole Indian ever owned me.
Q. Haven't you an enrollment in the Seminole Nation? A. Yes, sir my folks done it unbeknownst to me.
Q. Haven't you receive an allotment in the Seminole Nation? A. No sir, I don't

know nothing about it. I never have seen my land.

Q. Have you ever been enrolled in any other nation? A. No sir, they enrolled me on there.

(The name of the witness appears upon the final roll of the citizens of the Seminole Nation approved by the Secretary of the Interior on April 2, 1901, opposite No. 2739, as Betsey Mahardy, 57 years of age, and having been identified as a citizen of the Seminole Nation and a member of the Caesar Bruner Freedman Band. An allotment of the lands of the Seminole Nation was made to Betsey Mahardy in the year 1901.)

BY MR. APPLE:

Q. Did you ever make any application at the land office for any land? A. No, sir.

Q. You never made formal application for the allotment that was made to you in the Seminole Nation? A. No sir.

Q. Did you ever apply to the Dawes Commission for enrollment as a Seminole by blood or as a freedman? A. No sir, my folks done it unbeknownst to me.

Q. Who of your folks do you refer to? A. Ben Bruner's wife. She is a widow now.

Q. Is she a freedman or a Seminole? A. Seminole. I don't know whether she is living now or not.

Q. How was she related to you? A. She was my sister.

Q. Is she living now? A. I don't know. I haven't heard from her in a long time.

Q. Did you authorize her as your agent to make application for that land for you? A. No sir, I never have.

Q. You are the mother of the applicant Samuel Mahardy? A. Yes, sir.

Q. Who was his father? A. Wyatt Mahardy.

Q. When were you married to Wyatt Mahardy? A. I couldn't tell you when I was married to him.

Q. Fix the date as nearly as you can. A. I don't know about the date. I don't know the date of nothing. I never went to school, and never paid attention to nothing like that.

Q. Were you a slave before the war? A. Yes, sir.

Q. Were you married to Wyatt Mahardy before or after the Civil War? A. Before—no, during the war.

Q. The war was going on? A. Yes, sir.

Q. You said you made flight from the Creek country down south? A. Yes, sir, from the Creek country to the Seminole Country.

Q. Had you been married before that time? A. No, sir.

Q. Were you in the Seminole country when you married Wyatt Mahardy? A.

No, we had gone to the Chickasaw Nation.

Q. How long had you been in the Chickasaw Nation when you married Wyatt Mahardy? A. Two years.

Q. Are you positive the war was still going on when you married him? A. Yes, sir.

Q. Do you know when the soldiers returned from the war? A. No, sir I don't.

Q. Did you and Wyatt Mahardy have any other child older than Sam? A. No, sir.

Q. You did have one didn't you? A. Yes sir, older than Sam.

Q. Had you been married once before you married Wyatt? A. Yes, sir.

Q. Did you understand me a while ago when I asked you if you had ever been married before? A. No, I didn't understand.

Q. Who was your first husband? A. Bruner.

Q. Where were you living when you were married to him? A. In the Creek Nation.

Q. Was it before or after the war? A. Before.

Q. Did you have any children by Bruner? A. Yes sir, one.

Q. What is his name? A. Richard Bruner.

Q. Is he living? A. Yes, sir.

Q. Is he enrolled? A. On the Seminole Roll.

Q. Does he live in the Seminole Nation? A. No, he lives in the Chickasaw Nation.

Q. Do you know the date of Sam's birth? A. No, I don't.

Q. Do you know under what law you were married to Wyatt? A. Chickasaw.

Q. Did he have a Chickasaw license? A. Yes, sir he did.

Q. Have you that license now? A. No, we didn't have no license.

Q. Who married you? A. John Ishtone, a full blood.

Q. Was he a preacher or a judge? A. He was a preacher. He was a full blood, but he married white folks, Indians and colored folks.

Q. Was John Ishtone a full blood Chickasaw Indian? A. Yes, sir.

Q. Did he give you a certificate? A. No, sir.

Q. Never gave you a paper of any sort? A No, sir.

Q. Where were you living at the time? A. In the Chickasaw Nation.

Q. Where were you at the time you were married—were you at your home, or a church, or where? A. At John Ishtone's home.

Q. Where did he live? A. On Rock Creek.

Q. What direction is that from where you live? A. Toward Mill Creek.

Q. South of you? A. No, east.

Q. Did you continue to reside in the Chickasaw Nation? A. Yes, sir.

Q. You reside there, still? A. Yes, sir.

> Q. Have you never lived anywhere else? A. No sir.
>
> Q. Did you raise Sam? A. Yes, sir.
>
> Q. In the Chickasaw Nation? A. Yes sir.

The interview continued for several more pages. During that interview, it was revealed that Wyatt Mahardy was now deceased, and had passed only a few months before. And also, a very interesting exchange occurred about whether Betsey was Creek or Seminole. She explained how at the time the war began, she was visiting her sister who was Seminole, then they all had to leave and go south into Chickasaw country to avoid the war. She was adamant of her identity as Creek.

Questions were then posed about her son by her first marriage, and she explained how she was married to a Seminole, which then brought an interesting exchange and brought about the questions of her marriage, from the commissioner:

> Q. Were you a slave to Bruner during the war? A. Yes, sir, till they set them all free.
>
> Q. Till the slaves were emancipated? A. Yes, sir.
>
> Q. Now you said your first husband was a man named Bruner. Was he a slave? A. No, sir.
>
> Q. Was you ever married to Bruner or did he just live with you? A. Yes, sir, I was married to him. He was an Indian.
>
> Q. What do you mean by saying you was a slave and married to this Indian? A. Indians has slaves.
>
> Q. You said you were married to Bruner who was an Indian? A. I married him.
>
> Q. You had one child by Bruner? A. Yes, sir.
>
> Q. What was his name? A. Richard Bruner.
>
> Q. Is Richard living now? A. Yes sir.
>
> Q. How old a man is Richard? A. He is 45.

Later there was more curiosity about her first Seminole husband.

> Q. What became of your first husband? A. He went to the north and died.
>
> Q. When did he die? A. I don't know. So long time, I don't know.
>
> Q. Was he dead when you married Mahardy? A. Yes sir, of course. I wouldn't marry till I heard he was dead and know he was dead.
>
> Q. Was anybody present at the time you married Wyatt Mahardy? A. Yes, sir, but they are all dead. I couldn't tell you who was there. A whole lot of Indians was there.

A very strong statement of support for Samuel Mahardy appears in the file; this statement came from John Thomas, a Chickasaw by blood. He confirmed much of what Betsey had said about their coming into Chickasaw country during the war. He also confirmed that Samuel had attended Chickasaw schools and had boarded with him while going to that school. He confirmed that Mahardy was always viewed as being Chickasaw. He also confirmed that Wyatt Mahardy had received payments on behalf of the boy Samuel, while Samuel was attending school, and that he, John Thomas, had witnessed Wyatt Mahardy receiving the payments. Clearly, the file in its entirety is worth reading and examining.

The interview with Samuel Mahardy himself is most revealing. He tells a fascinating story about himself, his childhood, and his identity as a Chickasaw. Having once been given land as a Seminole Freedman, he returned the certificates awaiting correction or adjustment to his status as being Chickasaw.

He confirmed a close family relationship, and he described how his father collected Chickasaw money on his behalf, and pointed out how his father once purchased red boots for him and a fine saddle for his mother. And the strongest statement by Mahardy and how he identified himself appears when the questioning went back to his status as a Seminole. He interrupted the questioner and made a powerful statement:

> Q. About the Seminole business—A. There was an old gentleman asked me about the Seminole money. He said, "When are you going into the Seminole Nation?" and I said I never will.
>
> Q. Was he an officer? A. No, he was a Bruner—the old lady's brother-in-law. He said I belonged over there and I said I didn't. He said, "They are going to pay out some money over there and if you don't come over, you won't get it." I said I didn't claim anything over there and I said I didn't need their money and wouldn't accept it. My mother sent me to Wewoka once to get her money. I was talking to Mr. Brown, and I said, "I claim a right over in the Chickasaw Nation, and don't want any in the Seminole Nation."

Samuel explained the confusion of how he came to seen as Seminole and his objection to this from his early years and his insisting on his strong identity as Chickasaw.

The young Mahardy recalled how Chickasaw officials came to their home and even spent the night there, took down the names of the family, and he would later learn that their names were stricken from the Chickasaw rolls. Clearly the young Samuel wished to be officially recognized by the tribe where he lived, was a part of his entire life, and was adamant about his being recognized by the officials as part of the community in which he had been a member his entire life.

There were many additional pages in this enormous file, but the final decision was not made in Samuel Mahardy's favor. His name remained on the Seminole rolls and not the Chickasaw, although that was where he felt that he had always belonged. This sentiment about his tribal connection was shared by many also in the Chickasaw community.

Many times, one will notice that the issue of whether one is "Indian" or not frequently arose. In this case, clearly Samuel Mahardy was Chickasaw, not only by blood, but by culture and identity. Yet, he was treated differently because of the "Negro" blood from a grandfather. The current practice of the day was to insure that a perceived "stain" from African blood would be his identity, thus enforcing a racially influenced policy of racial "superiority" and a racist policy of declaring a degree of "inferiority" to be placed on having an African presence in the bloodline.

Betsey would remain on the Seminole roll also, though she stated that she was Creek and not Seminole. The nations were clearly close to each other geographically and contact among people was fluid. The Mahardy family is clearly a family with blended cultures, bloodlines, and tribal histories. Theirs is one that reflects a true "melting pot" that was the life of many such families in Indian Territory, and it can be studied from many perspectives. The Mahardy legacy is richly rooted in multiple tribes, and is one that exemplifies the complexity of life in a pre-statehood land that would eventually become the state of Oklahoma.

Land allotment record from the case of Betsey Mahardy.

Fanny Turner and Family

There are many challenges when researching Oklahoma-based families, especially those coming from the various bands within the Seminole Nation. The research can be even more challenging when researching Seminole Freedmen. There are some good records, and thankfully there are enrollment cards to examine, but when it comes to the application jackets and interviews, the files are quite slim and many interviews are in fact not in the file.

However, there are other record types to explore and from which stories can be told. An example is found in the file of Fanny Turner, of Earlsboro, Indian Territory. Fanny and her husband, Tom Turner, lived on the edge of Indian Territory with their family in Earlsboro in the Oklahoma Territory. Also living with Fanny were her other children from previous marriages—Jesse Brown and Nora Bruner. In addition their two youngest children, Eva and Crisella, were also in the house. They are all enrolled on Seminole Freedman card number 651, Field number 44.

Front of Seminole Enrollment Card #651, Field #44.

Because Fanny was a young woman at the time, she was born many years into freedom, but on the reverse side of the card, it is noted that her mother, Dinah Walker, had once been enslaved by Seminole Short Bird. Her father was Caesar Payne, and it appears that he was not enslaved at all, for he too was born after the war.

When researching Seminole families the *tribal band* is the method of identifying persons who were citizens of the tribe. Fanny was a member of the Caesar Bruner band. Her father Caesar was a member of the Dosar Barkus band, and her mother was a member of the Bruner band, like Fanny. And all her children were Bruner band members. Note that her husband was a U.S. citizen and not enrolled in any of the tribes.

Back of Seminole Enrollment Card #651, Field #44.

The Application Jacket

The application jacket usually contains interviews of the applicants. Unfortunately there were only a few scant handwritten notes among papers including one birth affidavit for Fanny's youngest child, Crisella. Though they did contain some good information, the missing interview could have provided more about the family itself.

The file itself however, did not contain an interview of any kind. Like many files among Creeks, it turns out that many of the Seminole files, especially Freedmen interviews, are also missing. Among many of the microfilmed records are images of the outside jacket simply with the word "empty" written on the file cover. This can make the research extremely challenging.

In the case of Fanny Turner's family, one small note simply contained the names of Fanny's immediate family.[34] But also contained in the application jacket was a birth record, and certainly the family that descends from Fanny Turner will be encouraged to find the birth record of Crisella, Fanny's youngest child.[35] For some reason there were several images reflecting the birth of Crisella, as the image was apparently duplicated. And unfortunately there was no official Dawes interview for Fanny about her life and her family.

In cases such as these, it is important to treasure the one or two documents that might remain in the file, since the interview that may have occurred was either not transcribed or possibly was removed from the file. There is no indication that an official interview for Fanny ever occurred. With other tribes, one might occasionally see a summary of the official interview, but not the case with Fanny. As a result the page with the data on daughter Crisella's birth will be most valuable.

---

[34] *Seminole Freedman File 651*. National Archive Microfilm Publication M1301 Accessed from Fold3.com.
[35] Ibid.

Application for Seminole Citizenship of Crisella Turner.

To find out more about Fanny and her family, or her family's history it was necessary to re-examine the enrollment card to see if there might be other resources with more information about the family history. Finding more information would require re-examining all resources, in addition to expanding the search in other directions. In this case it was necessary to take three steps to find more data on the family:

1) Re-examine the enrollment card.
2) Analyze the land allotment records to find more data.
3) Find the family in the Federal census or other records.

1. Re-examining the enrollment card.

The back side of Freedmen enrollment cards always contains additional information. The names of the parents are reflected, and if the parents were enslaved the name of the slaveholder is included. By analyzing the data on the card, we notice that there is nothing suggesting that Fanny's parents had died, so there was a strong possibility that they were still living at the time, and therefore would have had a card of their own. Fanny's parents were Caesar Payne and Dinah Walker. I checked, and both did have enrollment cards.

Fanny's Father, Caesar Payne:

As it turns out, her father, Caesar Payne, was still living at the time of the Dawes enrollment, and there is a card reflecting a man called Caesar Payne as well. That particular Caesar was enrolled on Seminole Freedman card number 684. He resided in the town of Sasakwa. However, this Caesar Payne was only thirty-three years old. Fanny was twenty-three at that time. With only a difference of ten years between them, most likely this Caesar Payne was not her father.

Fanny's Mother, Dinah Walker

As was noted, Fanny's mother was indeed alive during the years of the Dawes Commission. She was a member of the Dosar Barkus band, and she was at that time married to a "states" man called Eugene Walker.[36] Her husband before Walker was Jim Bennett, who was deceased. Dinah's parents were Mack (no last name given) and Maria Foster, of the Dosar Barkus band, and were enslaved by Seminole Geo. Cloud.

There is much more to study and more people to research based on data from this card. Dinah's descendants extend into multiple families. The story of Fanny Turner's extended family is complex and full of data.

Front of Seminole Enrollment Card #650.[37]

---

[36] The term "states" man or often "state Negro" is a term used to describe people of color who came into the Indian Territory from the United States, and who were not born in Indian Territory. Often people who migrated from nearby Arkansas, Texas, Louisiana, and other southern states were referred to simply as "state Negroes."

[37] Year: 1910; Census Place: Econtuchka, Seminole, Oklahoma; Roll: T624_1274; Page: 12B; Enumeration District: 0183; FHL microfilm: 1375287. (Accessed on Ancestry.com.)

Back of Seminole Enrollment Card #650.

2. Analyzing the Land Allotment Applications

The decision to study the allotment applications also proved to be very successful. Although the Application jacket for Fanny was missing an interview, a two-page interview with Fanny Turner was found in the land allotment file! Useful information about her, where she lived and with whom, as well as issues about the land itself was contained in that file.

DEPARTMENT OF THE INTERIOR
COMMISSION TO THE FIVE CIVILIZED TRIBES
SEMINOLE LAND OFFICE
WEWOKA, I. T., JULY 1ST 1901

IN MATTER OF THE APPLICATION OF Fanny Turner to take allotments of land in the Seminole Nation for herself and her children, Jesse Brown, Nora Bruner, Eva and Crisella Turner, accompanied by a proper description of the lands applied for, the names of said parties being found on the Seminole Roll, approved by the Secretary of the Interior April 2nd, 1901 at Numbers 2021, 2022, 2023, 2024, and 2025 respectively.

FANNY TURNER being first duly sworn testified as follows:

BY THE COMMISSION:

Q. What is your name? A. Fanny Turner

Q. What is your post office address? A. Earlsboro, O. T.

Q. Are you a citizen of the Seminole Nation? A. Yes, sir.

Q. What band do you belong to? A. Caesar Bruner.

Q. Are you married? A. Yes, sir.

Q. Is your husband a citizen of the Seminole Nation? A. No, sir.

Q. Is he a citizen of any Indian Nation? A. No sir, he is a citizen of the United States.

Q. Have you or any other person named in this application ever made application before this time to this Commission to file on land, either in the Seminole Nation, or any other Indian nation? A. No, sir.

Q. Have you or any other persons named in this application ever made application before this time to this Commission to be enrolled as citizens of any other Indian nation? A. No, sir.

Q. Are all of the persons named in this application now living? A. Yes, sir.

Q. For whom are you selecting your home? A. Myself.

Q. Are you in actual possession of the lands named in this application? A. Yes sir.

Q. You make application for yourself for the east half and north west quarter of Section 2, Township 9, Range 5, containing 120 acres, is that correct? A. Yes, sir.

Q. Are there any improvements on this tract of land? A. Yes, sir.

Q. Is there a house on it? A. Yes, sir.

Q. Who lives in the house? A. I do.

Q. How many acres under cultivation on this land? A. 60 acres.

Q. Is the improved land fenced? A. Yes, sir.

Q. Does anyone else claim this land or any part of it? A. No, sir.

Q. Has anyone else any improvements on this land? A. No, sir.

Q. Have you been over and examined this land with a view to making this application for it? A. Yes, sir.

Q. Is it prairie or timber land? A. Prairie land

Q. You make application for your son Jessee Brown for the east half of the north west quarter and Lot 2 of Section 10, Township 9, Range 5, containing 120.56 acres, is that correct? A. Yes, sir.

Q. Are there any improvements on this tract of land? A. Yes, sir.

Q. Is there a house on it? A. Yes, sir.

Q. Who lives in the house? A. A man by the name of England. My renter.

Q. Does he live there under contract with you? A. Yes, sir.

Q. How many acres under cultivation on this land? A. 40 acres.

Q. Is the improved land fenced? A. Yes, sir.

Q. Does anyone else claim this land or any part of it? A. No sir.

Q. Has anyone else any improvements on it? A. No, sir.

Q. Have you been over and examined this land with a view to making this application for it? A. Yes, sir.

Q. Is it prairie or timber land? A. Prairie land.

Q. You make application for your daughter Nora Bruner for the east half and north west quarter or the north east quarter of Section 10, Township 9, Range 5, containing 120 acres is that correct? A. Yes, sir.

Q. Are there any improvements on this tract of land? A. Yes, sir.

Q. Is there a house on it? A. Yes, sir.

Q. Who lives in this house? A. Mose Turner, my renter.

Q. Does he live there under contract with you? A. Yes, sir.

Q. How many acres under cultivation on this land? A. 40 acres.

Q. Is the improved land fenced? A. Yes, sir.

Q. Does anyone else claim this land or any part of it? A. No, sir.

Q. Has anyone else any improvements on it? A. No, sir.

Q. Have you been over and examined this land with a view to making application for it? A. Yes, sir.

Q. Is it prairie land or timber land? A. Prairie land.

Q. You make application for your daughter Eva Turner for the east half of the south east quarter of Section 3 and the south west quarter of the south west quarter of Section 2, Township 9, Range 5, containing 120 acres is that correct? A. Yes, sir.

Q. Are there any improvements on this tract of land? A. Yes, sir.

Q. Is there a house on it? A. Yes, sir.

Q. Who lives in this house? A. Ben Jenkins, my renter.

Q. Does he live there under contract with you? A. Yes, sir.

Q. How many acres under cultivation on this land? A. About 40 acres.

Q. Is the improved land fenced? A. Yes, sir.

Q. Does anyone else claim this land or any part of it? A. No, sir.

Q. Has anyone else any improvements on it? A. No, sir.

Q. Have you been over and examined this land with a view to making application for it? A. Yes, sir.

Q. Is it prairie land or timber land? A. Prairie and a little timber on the creek.

Q. You make application for your daughter Crisella Turner for the west half of the south east quarter of Section 3, and Lot 1 of section 10, all of Township 9, Range 5 containing 120.79 acres is that correct? A. Yes, sir.

Q. Are there any improvements on this tract of land? A. Yes, sir.

Q. Is there a house on it? A. No, sir.

Q. How many acres under cultivation on this land? A. Twenty acres.

Q. Is the improved land fenced? A. Yes, sir.

Q. Does anyone else claim this land or any part of it? A. No, sir.

Q. Has anyone else any improvements on it? A. No, sir.

Q. Have you been over and examined this land with a view to making application for it? A. Yes, sir.

Q. Is it prairie or timber land? A. Prairie land.

Q. Will you accept these lands for yourself and children named herein as final allotments in the Seminole Nation? A. Yes, sir.

WITNESS:

F. J. Horn

Fanny (her X mark) Turner

L. R. Trubman (?)

Fred T. Morray (?)

Death record for Fanny Turner from Application Jacket.

This interview was detailed and provided great information about the family. There was discussion about the improvements made on the land, and so much more. It also revealed that there were renters living upon the same land where Fanny and her husband and children lived. In addition, one critical piece of information was contained in that file. According to a death notice found in the jacket, she died in September 1904, before receiving her allotment.

3. Examining Census and other records

The Federal census also reflected the Turner family living in the Seminole Nation, in 1900. Husband, Tom, Fanny, and the others are reflected there also.

1900 U.S. Census of Seminole Nation, Indian Territory.

And in 1910 the family is found now in the new state of Oklahoma which joined the union in 1907. Fanny was now deceased, and Tom is reflected as a widower in that census year. By 1910, he was most likely living upon the land allotment of the family as his late wife and children were all members of the Barkus band. Both census years point out that Tom was a citizen of the U.S. and not any of the tribes of Oklahoma, as he was born originally in Texas.

1910 U.S. Census of Seminole Nation, Oklahoma.

This file is a clear example of how extensive research can reveal many details about an ancestor's life when upon first glance the file is small. By re-examining the enrollment card two additional enrollment cards were found leading to the names of more ancestors for this family. In addition, an examination of the enrollment cards also reveals that extended families and children from previous relationships are present and that can show how many families overlap in the same region.

This family is a strong Seminole family with strong Seminole identity being reflected in both the Barkus and the Bruner bands. In addition, their family did not live in isolation, because some of the family members had spouses in the Creek Nation. There is much more that can be gleaned from the Turner family of the Seminole Nation. Hopefully these records will encourage Turner descendants to study more of its rich history. And in spite of the fact that the interview was not kept in the file, it is clear that more information about the Turner family was found.

Thankfully, Fanny was interviewed for her land allotment before she passed away. We hope her descendants lived on their allotment for many years, and were able to thrive and build a life as statehood eventually came and a new chapter began.

Benjamin Bruner and Family

From the Seminole Nation comes a case that clearly illustrates how important it is to go beyond the one document. Benjamin F. Bruner lived in the Seminole Nation most of his life. His mother came from Florida and his father was Creek. He was enrolled on Seminole Freedman card number 828, and his name was the only name on the card. He was a member of the Caesar Bruner band. By his age on the card he was old enough to have been born enslaved, but it is clearly indicated on his enrollment card that he was born free. He had also been known previously as Ben Bruner, and a note on the front of the card reflects that notation. Ben Bruner lived in the community of Econtuchka, in the Seminole Nation.

Front of Seminole Enrollment Card #828.

Because his name was the only name on the card, only one line of additional data was revealed, but it is still significant. It is revealed that his father was John Bruner who had been enslaved by James Factor. His mother's name was Grace Bruner, and she had been born free. It would be the free status of his mother that would have given him his own status as a free man as well. Both parents were part of the Bruner band, and both were deceased by the time he was making his application.

Back of Seminole Enrollment Card #828.

Bruner's status as free born was not unusual in the Territory. Generally, tribal citizens who had a parent who was free; that usually meant that the mother was the free citizen. The free status of the mother then allowed the passing of her "free" status to her children. Such was the case with Ben Bruner. His father was enslaved as noted on the card. However, in spite of having never been enslaved, he was still given the status as "Freedman" though he had never been "freed," having never been enslaved. This is the complexity of life in the Territory, where southern policies of treating all persons who had African ancestry differently. Ben Bruner was born free and his mother was never enslaved, yet he was categorized as a "Freedman" and placed on the roll as such.

The Application Jacket

Unfortunately, no application jacket for Benjamin Bruner exists. Like many of the records from the Seminole Nation, many simply do not exist and were never microfilmed and therefore never preserved. One might think that with so little data from the Dawes records, that there might not be much more to find. But there was still much more to his life and much more to discover.

An Obituary Opens the Door

Thankfully, an obituary from 1939, saved by a descendant of Benjamin Bruner leads to the story of a fascinating man. With this obituary and more research, additional information emerged, about a man who lived well into the twentieth century.

Obituary

Benjamin F. Bruner, Founder of "Brunertown" Succumbs After Long Illness
Seminole Freedman Born Eleven Years Before Emancipation
Oklahoma Eagle, Saturday June 10, 1939

With the passing of Benjamin F. Bruner, 87 year old Seminole Freedman and founder of "Brunertown," last week, Oklahoma lost another one of her native sons whose activities during the territorial days contributed to the colorful history of the state.

Bruner died May 31 at the family home in Holdenville. Funeral services were held at the Mt. Zion Baptist church in Seminole, Sunday June 4. The body was interred at Turkey Creek Cemetery. Bruner was born on the banks of the Washita River a few miles from Calvin eleven years before freedom. His mother and father were natives of the Indian Country. As a boy he attended the missions set up by white church goers for the education of Negroes and Indians.

Soon after the Civil War, the Bruner family founded "Brunertown" a community that still bears the name of the founder. Shortly afterwards, Bruner then a young man married Jeanetta Shields and to this union were born 3 children. In 1880, Bruner and his wife separated and he entered Hampton Institute in Virginia, where he studied for five years. Returning to the territory in 1885 he taught school and 1890 when he married Ellen Rentie. Six children were born to this union.

After his second marriage, Bruner established a home on his freedom allotment nears [sic] Earlsboro where he lived for fifteen years. During that time he served as a member of the Seminole Indian Council. In 1905 he moved to Holdenville, then an open country, where he became a "land baron" controlling 640 acres, representing an allotment to his wife and children. On this allotment, Bruner built a $9000 home which was included among Oklahoma's land marks as long as it stood. For the sharecroppers and other Negroes in the section he built a school. He donated the land and then built the Unity Baptist church, although he had joined the Presbyterian church at Hampton, he had never been baptized, and it was one of the pleasurable moments to recall his baptism in the church he built. He served continuously on the deacon board of that church. Survivors are a wife, Ellen Bruner, Holdenville; two sons, Jack Bruner, Seminole, and Edgar Bruner, Holdenville; three daughters, Ivory Hampton, Okmulgee, Leona Corbett and Edna Steward, Tulsa; a brother, Tom J. Bruner, Holdenville; a sister, Annie Payne, Seminole.

Obituary courtesy of Charles Gibson, Great Grandson of Benjamin Bruner

This portion of the rich Bruner family history is that of a man born into the Seminole Nation, whose mother was a Seminole by blood and whose father was enslaved by a Creek Indian. He lived most of his life in the Seminole Nation, but was educated at a mission school for Indians and former slave children. He also attended Hampton Institute for a while before returning to his native Oklahoma. Was he among the Indian students who attended Hampton Institute? That is not clear, nor known, but it is clear that education was important to him.

Although the mission school he attended was not mentioned, there is a strong chance that he attended the Tullahassee Manual Labor School, located in the Muskogee area, or the Creek Seminole College in Boley, Oklahoma, or a third option—Evangel Mission, also in Muskogee.

More About Ben Bruner

More details about his life and family were also found in his interview that is part of the University of Oklahoma Western History Collection and part of the Indian Pioneer Papers. These interviews were conducted in the 1930s, and Ben was interviewed by Nettie Cain from his home in Holdenville, Oklahoma. We also note that he was part of the Bruner clan that formed the Caesar Bruner band. Caesar Bruner was, in fact, his uncle. Another uncle was Creek Freedman Paro Bruner (referred to as Perry in the interview).

Also, examining his Dawes card, it only contained basic information about him. It was indicated that his mother was a Seminole by blood, yet this was not considered by the Dawes commissioners. So, in spite of his blood tie to his Seminole mother, and the contributions to the tribe and his presence for decades as a citizen, he was placed on the Freedman Roll.

Creek Seminole College, Boley, Indian Territory (now Oklahoma).
Courtesy Oklahoma Historical Society.

His interview in the 1930s for the Indian Pioneer project provides an interesting glimpse into his life.[38]

BEN F. BRUNER
INTERVIEW
#12836

Nettie Cain
January 24, 1938

Interview with Ben F. Bruner
Route 5, Holdenville Oklahoma

I was born August 2, 1852 on the banks of the South Canadian River near Ft. Holmes and the old government bridge.

My father John Bruner was a Creek Freedman who came from Alabama, and my mother Grace Bruner was a full blood Seminole who came from Florida with the Seminole Indians.

Father was a slave and was sold to Jim Factor for $3000 in Confederate money. Mother and we children were not slaves but Father's master allowed him to take his family when he was sold.

During the Civil War we went to the Chickasaw Nation and his master would let him rent land and would give him part of what he made.

Father and one older brother, with their families went south during the Civil War, while three other brothers, Perry, Cesar, and Will went North with the Seminole Indians and served with the Union Army until the close of the war.

Jim Factor, the big slave owner was a major in the Civil War under Col. John Jumper. Jim was very kind and good to his slaves.

After the close of the war, our family returned to the Pottawatomie country near Shawnee. Father had an ox team and wagon. Soon after we returned the Government gave us rations, as we were all in destitute circumstances. They gave us flour, corn and beef, but these rations were only issued once a year. The

Government soon began paying $15.00 for each member of the family and we stopped getting rations. The Freedmen shared in government payments the same as the full-blood Indians and they were also given allotments.

As he mentioned in the interview above, he was able to secure land, and his land records reflecting his selection of land are reflected in the interview below.[39]

DEPARTMENT OF THE INTERIOR
COMMISSION TO THE FIVE CIVILIZED TRIBES
SEMINOLE ALLOTMENT OFFICE
WEWOKA, I. T. September 20, 1901[40]

IN THE MATTER OF THE APPLICATION OF Ben Bruner to take an allotment of land in the Seminole Nation for himself, accompanied by a proper description of the land applied for, the name of said party being found upon the Seminole Roll approved by the Secretary of the Interior, April 2, 1901 at Number 2705.

Ben Bruner being duly sworn testified as follows:

BY THE COMMISSION:
Q. What is your name? A. Ben Bruner.
Q. What is your post-office address? A. Econtuska, O. T.
Q. Are you a citizen of the Seminole Nation? A. Yes, sir.
Q. What band to you belong to? A. Caesar Bruner.
Q. Are you married? A. Yes sir.
Q. Is your wife a citizen of the Seminole Nation? A. No, sir.
Q. Have you ever before this time made application to this Commission to file on any land either in the Seminole Nation or any other Indian Nation? A. No, sir.
Q. Have you ever before this time made application to be enrolled in any other Indian Nation? A. No sir.
Q. Do you own a home in the Seminole Nation? A. Yes, sir.
Q. Are you filing on your home place in this application? A. Yes, sir.
Q. Are you in actual possession of the land named in this application? A. Yes,

---

[39] National Archives Publication M1186, Enrollment Cards.

[40] Ancestry.com, Oklahoma and Indian Territory, *Land Allotment Jackets for Five Civilized Tribes, 1884-1934*. [database on-line] Provo, UT, USA: Ancestry.com Operations, Inc, 2014.

sir.

Q. You make application for yourself for the SE ¼ of NE 1/4 and W ½ of the NE ¼ of NE ¼ of NE ¼ of Sec 27, T 11, R 5 containing 60 acres, is that correct? A. Yes, sir.

Q. Are there any improvements on this land? A. Yes, sir.

Q. Is there a house on it? A. Yes, sir.

Q. Does anyone else claim this land or any part of it? A. No, sir.

Q. Who lives in this house? A. Myself.

Q. How many acres under cultivation? A. Fifty acres.

Q. Is the improved land fenced? A. Yes, sir.

Q. Has anyone else improvements on this land? A. No sir.

Q. Have you been over the land and examined it with a view of making this application for it? A. Yes, sir.

Q. Is it prairie land or timber land? A. It is timber land.

Q. Will you accept this land for yourself as your final allotment in the Seminole Nation? A. Yes, sir.

Ben Bruner

Subscribed and sworn to me this the 20th day of September, 1901 at Wewoka, Indian Territory.

Fred T. Horry (?)
NOTARY PUBLIC

The Bruner family is a distinguished one with a detailed and rich history. It is evident that the family remembers his legacy, and that the story of Benjamin Bruner is not forgotten. Clearly his story can still be told and shared.

The Family of Clara and Paro Cudjo

This Cudjo family from Wewoka is a family like others in Indian Territory, that can be considered one that is a truly "blended family," as the mother and children are Seminoles and the father was Creek. In the case of Clara Cudjo and her children, she appeared in front of the Dawes Commission to enroll herself, her daughter Peggie, and her four stepchildren, Bettie, Peter, Jack, and Morris. Her husband was Paro Cudjo, who was a citizen of the Creek Nation. Clara was a member of the Dosar Barkus band of Seminoles.

Her father was Daily Davis, who was once enslaved by Bill Coody. His mother was Peggy who was also enslaved by Coody. Clara's husband, Paro Cudjo, was Creek and was once enslaved by Barney Thlocco. The mother of the stepchildren was Belle Cudjoe, who was deceased by the time of the Dawes Commission.

Front of Seminole Enrollment Card #820.

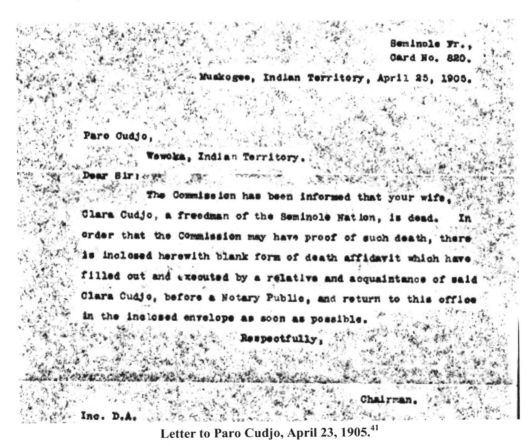

Back of Seminole Enrollment Card #820.

Application Jackets

Unfortunately, many of the Seminole interviews, like the Creek Interviews, are missing or incomplete, and were not well preserved. Some are not labeled correctly, and others are simply missing. Detailed files do not exist for many of the corresponding enrollment Dawes Cards. Thankfully, there was a file that contained one more document pertaining to Clara Cudjo. That one page however is significant, because it points out that Clara Cudjo herself apparently died before the rolls were closed.

Letter to Paro Cudjo, April 23, 1905.[41]

Nancy Davis was a sister of Clara Cudjo, and she appeared in order to make application on behalf of her sister Clara, now deceased. Clara's data of death was said to have been October 10, 1900.

---

[41] Ancestry.com, Oklahoma and Indian Territory, *Land Allotment Jackets for Five Civilized Tribes, 1884-1934.* National Archives Publication M1301.

DEPARTMENT OF THE INTERIOR
COMMISSIONER TO THE FIVE CIVILIZED TRIBES
SEMINOLE ALLOTMENT OFFICE
WEWOKA, I. T. October 19, 1901

IN THE MATTER OF THE APPLICATION OF Nancy Davis to take an allotment of land in the Seminole Nation for her sister Clara Cudjo, deceased and accompanied by a proper description of the land applied for, the name of said party being found upon the Seminole Roll, approved by the Secretary of the Interior April 2, 1901 at Number 2670

Nancy Davis being first duly sworn testified as follows:

Q. What is your name? A. Nancy Davis
Q. What is your post office address? A. Wewoka, I. T.
Q. Are you a citizen of the Seminole Nation? A. Yes, sir.
Q. What band do you belong to? A. Dosar Barkus
Q. Are you married? A. No, sir.
Q. Have you ever before this time made application to this Commission for your sister Clara Cudjo, deceased to file on any land either in the Seminole Nation, or any other Indian Nation? A. No, sir.
Q. Is your sister Clara now living? A. No, sir.
Q. When did she die? A. She died the 10th day of October, 1900.
Q. Are you in actual possession of the land named in this application? A. No, sir.
Q. You make application for your sister Clara Cudjo, deceased, for the NW ¼ of the NW ¼ and the SE ¼ or the NW ¼ of Sec 14 and the SW ¼ of SE ¼ of Sec. 11, T 9, R 5, containing 120 acres, is that correct? A. Yes, sir.
Q. Are there any improvements on this land? A. No, sir.
Q. Is there a house on it? A. No, sir.
Q. Does anyone else claim this land or any part of it? A. No, sir.
Q. Has anyone else made improvements on this land? A. No, sir.
Q. Have you been over this land and examined it with a view of making application for it? A. Yes, sir.
Q. Is it prairie land or timber land? A. Prairie land.
Q. Will you accept this land for your sister Clara Cudjo, deceased as her final allotment in the Seminole Nation? A. Yes, sir.

NOTICE TO APPLICANT: You are advised that the allotment as selected by you for your sister Clara Cudjo, deceased, will be reserved for said deceased person until the Commission has finally determined the identity of the heirs to be entitled to share in said allotment.

WITNESS:
W. J. Hastain
Nancy (her X mark) Davis
Charles E. Webster

Subscribed and sworn to me this the 19th day of October, 1901 at Wewoka, Indian Territory.

Fred T. Marry
NOTARY PUBLIC

Another interview was also a part of the file, with Paro Cudjo, Clara's husband. Although she was identified as deceased, he was allowed to still appear and make a claim for the land that she was entitled to had she lived. On that document, we see the same questions pertaining to the status of the land, improvements upon the land, and the nature of the parcel of land.

Nancy Davis being first duly sworn testified as follows:

Q. What is your name? A. Paro Cudjo
Q. What is your post office address? A. Wewoka, I. T.
Q. Are you a citizen of the Seminole Nation? A. No, sir.
Q. Are you married? A. No, sir, my wife is dead.
Q. Was she a citizen of the Seminole Nation? A. Yes, sir.
Q. What band did she belong to? A. Dosar Barkus
Q. Have you ever before this time made application to this Commission for your wife Clara Cudjo, deceased to file on any land either in the Seminole Nation, or any other Indian Nation? A. No, sir.
Q. Have you ever before this time, made application to this Commission for your wife to be enrolled as a citizen of any other Indian nation? A. No, sir.
Q. Is your wife Clara Cudjo now living? A. No, sir.
Q. When did she die? A. In October, 1900.
Q. Are you in actual possession of the land named in this application? A. No, sir.
Q. You make application for your sister Clara Cudjo, deceased, for the NW ¼ of the NW ¼ and the SE ¼ of the NW ¼ of Sec 14 and the SW ¼ of SE ¼ of Sec. 11, T 9, R 5, containing 120 acres, is that correct? A. Yes, sir.

Q. Are there any improvements on this land? A. No, sir.

Q. Is there a house on it? A. No, sir.

Q. Does anyone else claim this land or any part of it? A. No, sir.

Q. Has anyone else made improvements on this land? A. No, sir.

Q. Have you been over this land and examined it with a view of making application for it? A. Yes, sir.

Q. Is it prairie land or timber land? A. Timber land.

Q. Will you accept this land for your wife Clara Cudjo, deceased as her final allotment in the Seminole Nation? A. Yes, sir.

NOTICE TO APPLICANT: You are advised that the allotment as selected by you for your wife Clara Cudjo, deceased, will be reserved for said deceased person until the Commission has finally determined the identity of the heirs to be entitled to share in said allotment.

WITNESS:

W. J. Hastain

Paro (his X mark) Cudjo

[illegible]

Subscribed and sworn to me this the 8th day of January, 1902 at Wewoka, Indian Territory.

Fred T. Marry

NOTARY PUBLIC

It is not known if the fact that there were two applications for Clara's land created conflict or whether rights were given to the husband by default. The remaining documents reflect the presence of the husband in the file, and nothing additional was known of Nancy's application. However, for research purposes, it is useful to know that there was a sister, and that the family has another name to follow and study, to expand the family narrative.

Another question arises pertaining to the family. What can be learned about Paro Cudjo himself? A search on two databases did not reveal the name of Paro Cudjo. Was he possibly related to Paro Bruner? After a thorough search it appears that they were not the same families. And Clara's card as well as the land records state that he was a Creek citizen. An examination was made with the name written as C-u-d-j-o-e, but no Paro Cudjoe there, either. It is not clear who ended up with the land from the documents, and it is not clear who Paro Cudjoe the father of her children, actually was. No enrollment card for Paro Cudjo exists, but clearly, the record does reflect his being Clara's husband and father of the children in the household.

With no enrollment card for Paro Cudjo, one might assume that he administered the estate for his deceased wife and that was the end of the story. However, some additional records pertaining to Clara's estate and her husband's status as administrator were found. Among the probate records of Oklahoma some additional records were located. The file was much larger than expected and eighteen more pages about Clara's property were located among probate records located on Ancestry.com. And on one record, Paro clearly revealed that he had lived on the land since Clara's death and that some improvements had been made over time. He pointed out that he had not rented the land to anyone, but he and the family had resided there.

Report in Probate of Administrator for Estate of Clara Cudjo.

But surprisingly there was a challenge to Paro Cudjo having been pointed as Administrator of her estate. It is not clear why there was a challenge, but it is clear that a challenge to his administrative status was made. It was recommended that Paro Cudjo not be allowed to continue as administrator of the estate of Clara and her children. The letter appears to be one from a company requesting that the bond be canceled pertaining to the status of Paro Cudjo as administrator. The company was requesting to be removed from any liability pertaining to the claim. It is not clear whether or not this was a technicality or if there was another issue at hand.

Being enrolled as a Creek, he would have received his sixty-acre allotment, and being married to Clara, their children would have also received allotments as Seminole citizens, so this family would have had many opportunities to explore life as now citizens of Oklahoma, as landowners, and as people in charge of their own destiny.

But with more than the spouse claiming the allotment for Clara, was this an effort to capture the land? It is known that many citizens of the Five lost their land due to many challenges put them in the early 1900s. It is not known if this was the case, or if Paro kept the land for some time.

In the 1910 Federal census three years after statehood, Paro, was living in the township of Lincoln, in Seminole County, with daughter Peggie, and another wife, Flora. His name was also found on some of the lesser known town rolls from the Creek Nation, but it is not clear why there does not appear to be an enrollment card for Paro Cudjo.

1910 United States Federal Census for Para Cudjo
Oklahoma › Seminole › Lincoln › District 0186

Name	Relation	Sex	Race	Marital S	Years Mar	Children	Children	Birthplace
Cudjo Paro	Head	m	B	53 m2	1			Oklahoma
— Flora	Wife	F	mu	54 m1	1	2	1	Oklahoma
— Peggie	Daughter	F	B	13 S				Oklahoma
Jacobs Joseph	Grandson	m	B	12 S				Oklahoma

Entry for the Paro Cudjo family, 1910 U.S. Census, Oklahoma.

Another Paro?

From Clara's card, her husband and the father of her children was Paro Cudjo, who had testified on Clara's behalf after her death. And he was alive when the Dawes Rolls had closed. And it was always pointed out that he was a Creek citizen. The fact that there is no card for him is a mystery. However, it appears that there was a card for another Paro with a different surname who was also Creek. And it appears that this Paro, may have actually have been *the* Paro Cudjo we are looking for.

By examining the Dawes Cards it was first necessary to study all people whose names were Paro Cudjo, and to enter as many names as possible in the database. When nothing clear came up, it was then necessary to examine all people in the Ancestry.com database with the surname of Cudjoe, or Cudjo. Since Paro emphasized that he was Creek, this was explored. Then it was decided to examine all Creek Freedmen called Paro—without a surname.

Paro Barnett

One card came up—Paro Barnett. With further examination, we noticed that there was a Paro Barnett. To be sure—that card was examined. *Paro Barnett was once enslaved by Barney Thlocco, the same slaveholder of Paro Cudjo.* There was also a small note on the card that said that Paro Barnett was on the 1895 Omitted Roll as Paro Cudjo. This was the clue that pointed out that Paro Barnett *was* Paro Cudjo.

Front of Creek Enrollment Card #45.

He was the son of Sam Cudjo and Vicey Barnett. It is clear that he later used the name of his father, and the name Barnett actually came from his mother, Vicey Barnett. She was also enslaved by Barnett Thlocco. Sam Cudjo, his father, was a Seminole, but Paro was not sure of who his father's slaveholder was.

Back of Creek Enrollment Card #45.

Thankfully, being able to solve the mystery of who Paro Cudjo was offers a new opportunity for additional research to be done on the family. Land allotment records will reflect the actual land, and there may be more that will document the history of this family. His ties to the Seminole Nation came not only through his wife, but also through his father. His mother, Vicey, was also still living at the time, leading to a bit more information that can be gleaned from the records.

Heirship Records Tell the Story

Within the Creek Nation another set of records contribute to the story of the family's history. The Creek Equalization Records are documents that prove heirship by descent for citizens of the Creek Nation. The database now available to the public contains data collected between 1912–1921. These records were created to equalize payments to equalize allotments made to individual Creeks.[42]

---

[42] The Heirship records are now available online through Ancestry.com.

In this case there was a record for Paro Barnett. This is the document that tells more of this family's history. An earlier marriage for Paro Barnett is shown, as was his marriage to Clara, and the names of the descendants of this family.

Creek Freedman File – Paro (Cudjo) Barnett.
Oklahoma Creek Equalization Records, 1912-1921.

Another page in this file also gives us the names of the parents and siblings of Paro Cudjo, and where they lived:

Name of Father and Mother		Age	Degree Indian Blood	D. C. Roll No.	Postoffice	Living or Dead	If Dead Give Date
Sam Cudjo,	Father.		Dead				
Wicey Cudjo,	Mother.		F'd'man 4693			Dead	

Name each brother and sister, whether living or dead and give the information called for in the blank forms. If half brother or sister state whether maternal or paternal.

Names of Brothers and Sisters	Brother or Sister	Age	Degree Indian Blood	D. C. Roll No.	Postoffice	Living or Dead	If Dead Give Date
Betty Grayson,	Sister					Dead	
Hillis Davis,	Sister					Dead	
Ned Cudjo,	Brother,				Wewoka, Okla.	Living,	
King Cudjo,	Brother,				"	"	
Perryman Cudjo,	Brother,				"	"	
Lucy Smith,	Sister.				Muskogee, Okla.	Living,	

State below if any deceased brothers or sisters had children. Name each one, whether living or dead and give the information called for in the blank form.

	Name of Child	Age	Degree Indian Blood	D. C. Roll No.	Postoffice	Living or Dead	If Dead Give Date
Joshua Cudjo — Name of Deceased Brother or Sister	Lesser Cudjo,	26	F'd'man		Wewoka, Okla.	Living,	

Creek Freedman File – Sam Cudjo.
Oklahoma Creek Equalization Records, 1912-1921.

Paro Cudjo Barnett's ties to the Creek Nation were strong, and it we noted earlier that he had also appeared on the Arkansas Colored Town roll several times in the 1890s, and he was with his family in another Township several years later. However the family ties to the Seminole Nation was equally strong and was well documented. Since Paro remained with the family on the same family land, we hope that the family thrived and continued their life within Seminole Country. We also hope that the short life of Clara Cudjo and the legacy of their family will be remembered well by the Cudjo descendants.

The Family of Delia Noble

From the story of Delia Noble and her family one learns the value of studying all categories of records from Indian Territory. Typically a researcher will use the standard enrollment cards, but the cards reflecting "New Borns" or "Minors" can be just as fruitful with the family's data. And sometimes one can begin with a New Born card that will point to other enrollment cards on a family.

With this family we begin with a Seminole New Born card, with three children, Stephen, Leford, and Rachel. All three children are five years or younger. Their mother is Delia Noble, and their father, George Noble, is said to be a Creek citizen. The family resided in Wewoka, Indian Territory, and it is clear that they have a rich tie to the nation. There is a notation that Stephen was also an applicant for enrollment as a citizen of the Creek Nation. We note that Stephen Noble's name was later crossed off the card, and a roll number was never placed beside his name.

Front of Seminole Freedman New Born Card #9, for the Noble children.

Delia, the mother of the children, was a Seminole, and her information is written on her own card. Her name and the names of additional children appear on Seminole Freedman card #648. On that card Delia Noble's name appears with the names of six other children. The children were Shake Payne, and William, Benjamin, Robert, Lyman, and Elbetta, all with the Noble surname. All whose names appear on this card are noted as members of the Bruner band.

Front of Seminole Enrollment Card #648, for Delia Noble.

Back of Seminole Enrollment Card #648, for Delia Noble.

It is also clear that the father, George Noble, is a Creek citizen as he is found on Creek Enrollment Card 1400, Field card 1516.

Front of Creek Enrollment Card 1400, Field card 1516, for George Noble.

On the back of the card, George Noble's history is revealed. His father was Scipio Holmes, a Seminole, and his mother Frances Holmes was Creek, from Canadian Colored Town. Noting the different surname of his father it is not known where the Noble surname originated.

Back of Creek Enrollment Card 1400, Field card 1516, for Scipio Holmes.

Application Jackets

Application jackets do not exist for either parent. There is not one for George Noble among the Creek files, nor is there one for Delia Noble among Seminole files. However, because there was a separate effort to enroll Stephen Noble as a Creek, the family story was still found. Stephen's name was put on a Seminole Enrollment Card (see above) among those cards known as "New Born" cards. Thankfully there is an extensive file to be found reflecting his status, with interviews pertaining to not only the family but their presence on earlier rolls.

Finding the Family's Data

Looking and finding data on the family was a challenge. For Seminole Enrollment Card number 648 no application jacket exists among the many digitized images found on Fold3.com nor on Ancestry.com.

Among the collections to be found are the categories of "Seminole," "Seminole Memorandum," "Seminole New Born," and "Seminole New Born Freedmen." And strangely, there is no single category of "Seminole Freedmen" to be found, and from the file of "Seminole New Born Freedmen" a file accompanies the card with the three children, Stephen, Leford, and Rachel. The greater surprise is that an extensive set of documents were contained within that file. It is from that file of the New Born Freedmen that an amazingly rich series of interviews and documents are found.

In addition, there were some birth affidavits of the children. Birth records are often found in the application jackets. These are valuable records because they provide information that pre-dates Oklahoma statehood and also the process of documenting births.

Many of the questions involved their status, and an effort was made to determine if they were Seminole or Creek. George Noble, in fact, had appeared in front of the commission in 1904 to enroll his son Stephen as a Creek. George explains how he was enrolling his son, and it was noted that Delia his wife was Seminole. Much of the questioning in the interview focused on whether or not George was registering only one child while the others were registered as Seminole. He explained himself several times, and he was challenged on whether he was accurate about the dates. He pointed out that he recorded dates of birth from the family bible, and he noted that he was registering the child Stephen because the others had been registered already as Seminoles.

DEPARTMENT OF THE INTERIOR
COMMISSION TO THE FIVE CIVILIZED TRIBES
MUSKOGEE, I. T. AUGUST 12, 1904

In the matter of the application for the enrollment of Stephen Noble as a Creek Freedman.

APPEARANCE: Mr. M. L. Mott, attorney for the Creek Nation

George Noble being sworn testified as follows:

Q. What is your name? A. George Noble
Q. How old are you? A. Forty two.
Q. What is your post office address? A. Wewoka.
Q. Do you make application for enrollment of Stephen Noble as a Creek Freedman? A. Yes sir.
Q. Are you his father? A. Yes, sir.

The records of the Commission show that George Noble is listed for enrollment on Creek Freedman Field Card No 1516, and that his name is contained in the partial list of Creek Freedmen approved by the Secretary of the Interior March 28, 1902, No 4920.
Q. Is Stephen Noble living? A. Yes, sir.

Q. What is the name of his mother? A. Delia Noble.

Q. Is she a citizen of the Seminole Nation? A. Yes, sir

The records of the Commission show that the name of Delia Noble appears on the approved Seminole Roll No. 2004.

Q. When was Stephen Noble born? A. I can see in a minute.

Q. Have you a record of it? A. Yes, sir. I put it down what month it was born; I have got the names down in a book at home; I never could think of it, so I just put it down; 1900, born June.

The applicant presents for inspection of the Commission a pocket memorandum book in which is found what purports to be a record of the date of birth of Stephen Noble.

Q. Did you do the writing in this book? A. Yes, sir.

Q. When did you write it in this book? A. I don't remember exactly when, but I don't that myself in the book; I don't remember when.

Q. You say you did this yourself? A. Yes, sir.

Q. Did you do it soon after this child was born? A. Yes, sir.

Q. In this book? A. Yes, sir.

Q. Have you gotten it written down in another? A. Yes sir, down in a bible but I didn't bring it with me; I just had the day book, here.

Q. Did you copy this from the bible? A. Yes, sir.

Q. When did you make that entry in the Bible about the date of birth? A. Just after he was born.

Q. Does this in this book give the same date that it does in the Bible? A. Yes, sir.

Q. Have you a child named Leeford? A. Yes, sir.

Q. When was that child born? A. 1902.

Q. What day and month? A. I can't tell you cause I never could keep track; I am short of recollection and the earliest way I can remember a thing is to put it down. Both of the children is right there.

Q. Is Stephen older than Leeford? A. Yes, sir.

Q. How much older? A. He must be two years older than Leeford.

Q. More than two, or less than two? A. About two years older.

The book which the applicant presents contains the following entries:
Stephen Noble born June the 15th 1900
Leeford Noble born May the 31, 1902

Q. Did your wife make an affidavit about the birth of Stephen? A. I believe she did.

Q. Were you with her when she made it? A. Yes, sir; I was over there.

Q. Are you positive that this date that you have here, gives the correct date of the birth of Stephen? A. Yes, sir.

Q. If your wife give a different date, she is mistaken, is she? A. She might be. That's the correct date from the one in the Bible, cause I seed the one in the bible when the child was born and I went a got a copy.

Q. The affidavit made by your wife states that the child was born on the 19th of June 1900; and you say the correct date is the 15th of June 1900? A. Yes, sir.

Examination by Mr. Mott:

Q. Have you got another child enrolled? A. In the Creek Nation?

Q. Yes. A. No sir.

Q. In any other nation? A. My oldest children are all enrolled in the Seminole Nation.

Q. Is your wife dead? A. No sir, she's living.

Q. You are a Creek citizen? A. Yes, sir.

Q. She a Seminole? A. Yes, sir.

Q. Where is she? A. She's up there about 4 miles northwest of Wewoka.

Q. How many children have you got? A. About 7.

Q. Why did you put Leeford Noble down here? A. I just wanted to put him down. He is the next one to Stephen.

Q. Why did you put only two down here, and not the others down? A. I didn't thought I would need to put them down; They had filed up there in the Seminole nation.

Q. Well there is not any need to put Leeford down; you knew he couldn't file didn't you? A. Yes, sir.

Q. When did you put these down? A. I don't know exactly. I wouldn't say because I am not positive when I did write it, but I written it in myself.

Q. About what time did you put it down, do you know? A. No sir, I don't.

Q. Has it been a year ago? A. I don't think it was a year, but what date I can't tell you.

Q. Was it six months? A. That's what I don't know, I keep telling you.

Q. Haven't you any idea when you put it down? A. No, sir.

Q. Well you put it down for the purpose of bringing it here for evidence didn't you? A. Yes, sir.

Q. And then can't tell whether you put it down 6 months of 12 months ago? A. I think it ain't 12 months ago; of course I don't know exactly what month I put it down and can't say.

Q. Well, to your best judgement? A. It can be much more than 2 months ago since I written in that book there.

Q. You put it down for the purpose of bringing it here as evidence? A. Yes, sir.

Q. Why didn't you bring it then? A. Well, I couldn't go off then; it was a good ways and money was hard to get and we come when we could.

Q. Why didn't you bring the Bible? A. I didn't think that was needed; That was more handy to fetch than the Bible.

Q. It is not as good evidence as the Bible. A. Well, the Bible could come, if, it is needed.

The most essential part of this application jacket is an on-going interview examining the status of the family. Keep in mind that the father in this household—George Noble—was a Creek Citizen and their mother, Delia, was Seminole. Much of the interview seems to ask the same questions again and again. An associate of George Noble was also called to verify the birth of the child, and the examination continued. At times there appeared to be an effort to confuse the witness George, pointing out statements that he had made earlier in response to previous questions.

Throughout the many pages in the interview, the questions continued also about his movement. The Commission seemed interested not only in how often he came to trade but also with whom he visited when coming to town to trade. The number of times George came to file on his land was discussed. The complexity of questions directed to applicants is clearly seen in this file. As much as some files were strangely brief or non-existent in many files, this case seemed to cover multiple angles about his desire to enroll his son.

The point is also that the questioning pertains to Creek enrollment, although George's wife and children were Seminoles of the Bruner band. While the ultimate status of the family would be that of a Seminole family, it is also important to realize how close these two tribes were as well. Families knew each other and mingled socially. Many from one tribe chose a spouse from the other tribe, and it is well known that both cultures share similar origins from the southeast. As witnesses were called, the reader can glean much about the process of Dawes enrollment, when often the line of questioning would stray from the status of the applicant and often focus on one or two details. However, the reader can also learn much about the movement and life of the applicant with some of the details expressed.

The file went on for multiple pages, and even beyond the question and answer interviews, twenty more pages were part of this massive file. Most of the questions were similar, in that they were basic questions about whether or not people knew George Noble closely and were asked if they had visited the Noble household and recalled the birth of the child Stephen. The Commissioners focused on the fact that there was movement when called to appear and register, and one can see how often people were responding to the call to enroll.

One associate was called and asked about his own child's date of birth, and whether or not George Noble's child was born before or after his child's birth. Delia is mentioned continually, and her status as Seminole was repeatedly mentioned. But it is Delia's own voice that appears to be missing. She was not a witness on these pages, yet, her presence and status as a Seminole was discussed, but never challenged.

Decision

The enrollment of Delia's other children was always that of their being Seminoles of the Bruner band. In 1907, a decision was finally made on the case for Stephen. The application to enroll him as a Seminole Freedman was denied. However the denial was based on the fact that he had been enrolled as a Creek and his status was therefore not changed, and he remained on the Rolls as a Creek Freedman.

Sem-Fr- NB-9

Muskogee, Indian Territory, April 16, 1907.

George Noble,
Wewoka, Indian Territory.

Dear Sir:

You are hereby advised that on February 19, 1907, the Secretary of the Interior affirmed the decision of the Commissioner to the Five Civilized Tribes, rendered January 7, 1907, denying the application for the enrollment of Stephen Noble as a citizen of the Seminole Nation.

Respectfully,
Commissioner

Chief Clerk of Seminole Enrollment Division,
Muskogee, Indian Territory.

Dear Sir:

Receipt is acknowledged of your letter of December 29, 1905, in which you ask to be advised as to the status of the application for the enrollment of Stephen Noble, son of George Noble, a Creek citizen, and Dilia Noble, a Seminole Freedman, as a citizen of the Creek Nation.

In reply you are advised that a decision, enrolling said Stephen Noble as a citizen of the Creek Nation, is now before the Commissioner for his approval and signature.

Respectfully,
[Illegible]
Commissioner

The extensive file for the Noble family reflects a complex and interesting history. We hope their story will be told of how one branch of the family was Creek, but that all except one of Delia's children were Seminole and that their strong legacy continues in both nations.

The Family of Hazen Dosar

The Dosar family of Mekasuka (Mikasukey) in Indian Territory was a Seminole family that lived closely with other extended family members for many years. Finding records reflecting their whole story was a challenge due to missing records. There are enrollment cards, but the accompanying records found in application jackets are simply missing and were never microfilmed by the National Archives. Thankfully the remaining records still reflect a rich family history.

Hazan Dosar was a young man who appeared in front of the Dawes Commission to enroll his wife Sarah and his stepsons Amos and Levi Warrior. His father was a man simply called Dosar, but who also was known as Sam Robert. His mother was Dotty Lotty, who was a member of the Bruner band of Seminole Freedmen. The entire family was part of the Bruner band.

Front of Seminole Enrollment Card #652, for Hazan Doser Family.

On the reverse side of the card, we learn more about Hazan Doser's background and the name of his father, Dose, and his mother, Dotty Lotty. Both were still living at the time, and although not much is known of Doser, the father, Dotty was a member also of the Bruner band.

Back of Seminole Enrollment Card #652, for Hazan Doser Family.

Hazen, the father, also had two children whose names were placed on a Seminole "New Born" card. His daughter Lethia Ann Doser was on "New Born" card number 83 and daughter Dollie was on card number 92. On the card that follows, one can see that Hazan Doser was a young man who was born in the years after the Civil War. Therefore he was born free and not enslaved.

Daughter Dollie's Card

A note from Hazan's enrollment card, indicated that another child was listed on the Seminole New Born Freedmen card #92. Her mother was Viola Dosar, and her father was Hazan. It is not clear whether Hazan had a previous marriage or whether this was another wife with whom Hazan had a relationship.

Front of Seminole Freedman New Born Card #92, for Dollie Dosar.

Daughter Leathia Ann's Card

Coming from Wewoka was another daughter, whose name was Leathia Ann Dosar. She is only one year old, and her mother was Lucy Sancho. Lucy is enrolled on her own card #813.

Front of Seminole Freedman New Born Card #83, for Leathia Ann Dosar.

Mother Dolly's Card

Not far away in Sasakwa, Hazan Dosar's mother Dollie was found. She appeared in front of the Dawes Commission enrolling only herself. Both of her parents were deceased, and she had been enslaved by John Jumper, the Seminole leader who was twice elected principal chief.

Front of Seminole Enrollment Card No 709, Field No 102, for Dolly Lotty.

Back of Seminole Enrollment Card No 709, Field No 102, for Dolly Lotty.

Application Jacket

There is no application jacket that survives for Hazan Dosar, but a jacket was found for the young daughter, Dollie Dosar.[43]

The file offers only a small glimpse into the family's history. Statements were taken from Hazan and Viola, mother of Dollie. Although there was no interview in the file, the enrollment of daughter Dollie as a Seminole New Born was ruled in her favor, and she was added to the roll as a New Born Seminole citizen. At the time of enrollment the mother was ill and was unable to enroll for her daughter as was pointed out in the sworn statements.

United States of America, Indian Territory)
     Western Judicial District   )

          Affiant Hazen Dosar, being of lawful age and first duly sworn, on his oath deposes and says: I am a freedman citizen of the Seminole Nation, above the age of twenty-one years, my wife's name is Viola Dosar; there was born to me and my wife, on the 16th day of September, A.D., 1902, a female child, which has been named Dollie Dosar; that said child is still living; that the reason why no application was made for the enrollment of said child while the land office was located at Wewoka, I.T., for the enrollment of new born Seminole children, is that the mother of said child was dangerously ill, and I was informed that applications could not be made by the father if the mother was living.

                                             H 8z Doro

                    Subscribed and sworn to before me, this the 28th day of August, A.D., 1905.

                                             John W. Willmott
                                                  Notary Public.

Statement of Hazen Dosar.

---

[43] Ancestry.com. *U.S., Native American Applications for Enrollment in Five Civilized Tribes, 1898-1914.* [database on-line]. Provo, UT, USA: Ancestry.com Operations, Inc., 2013.

United States of America, Indian Territory,
Western Judicial District.

Affiant, Viola Dosar, being of lawful age and
first duly sworn, on her oath deposes and says: I am a freedman
citizen of the Seminole Nation; my husband's name is Hazen Dosar;
there was born to me and my said husband, on the 16th day of September, A.D., 1902, a female child, which we have named Dollie Dosar; that said child is still living; that I was unable to make
application before the Dawes Commission for the enrollment of said
child as a new born citizen of the Seminole Nation while the office
was open at Wewoka, I.T., on account of dangerous illness; and my
husband made no application, being under the impression that I alone
could make the application.

Viola Dosar

Subscribed and sworn to before me, this the 28th
day of August, A.D., 1905.

John W. Willmott
Notary Public.

Statement of Viola Dosar.

United States of America, Indian Territory)
Western Judicial District.   )

Affiant, Dinah Johnson, states on oath, as fol-
lows: I am a freedman citizen of the Seminole Nation, above the
age of forty-five years; that I well know Hazen Dosar and his wife
Viola Dosar, freedmen citizens of the Seminole Nation; that I was
present on at their house on the 16th day of September, A.D., 1902,
when a female child was born to said Viola and Hazen Dosar; that
I acted as mid-wife at the birth of said child; that I am well acquainted with said child, which has been named Dollie Dosar; that
said child is still living.

Attest
Jno. W. Willmott

Dinah Johnson her X mark

Subscribed and sworn to before me, this the
28th day of August, A.D., 1905.

John W. Willmott
Notary Public.

Statement of Dinah Johnson.

Beyond the page reflecting the statements of Hazen Dosar, Viola Dosar, and Dinah Johnson, one finds the actual decision that was made pertaining to Dollie and her enrollment.

DEPARTMENT OF THE INTERIOR
COMMISSIONER TO THE FIVE CIVILIZED TRIBES

In the matter of the application for the enrollment of Dollie Dosar as a citizen of the Seminole Nation.

DECISION

It appears on the record herein that on August 30, 1905, application was made to the Commissioner to the Five Civilized Tribes for the enrollment of Dollie Dosar as a citizen of the Seminole Nation.

It further appears from the record herein, that said applicant was born on September 16, 1902, and is the child of Hazen Dosar, whose name appears as number 2026 upon the final roll of citizens of the Seminole Nation approved by the Secretary of the Interior April 2, 1901, and Viola Dosar who is not identified as a citizen of the Seminole Nation, or an applicant for rights therein, and that said applicant was living on March 4, 1905.

Section One of the Act of Congress approved April 26, 1906 (34 Stats., 137), provides

"That after approval of this Act, no person shall be enrolled as a citizen or freedman of the Choctaw, Chickasaw, Cherokee, Creek or Seminole tribes of Indians in the Indian Territory, except as herein otherwise provided, unless application for enrollment was made prior to December first, nineteen hundred and five, and the records in charge of the Commissioner to the Five Civilized Tribes shall be conclusive evidence as to the fact of such application."

I am therefore of the opinion that Dollie Dosar should be enrolled as a citizen of the Seminole Nation, under the provisions of the Act of Congress approved March 3, 1905 (33 Stats., 1070), and it is so ordered.

Tams Bixby
(His signature)
Commissioner

Muskogee, Indian Territory
Jan 12, 1907 (stamped)

So as the issue pertaining to Dollie's registration was resolved, there was more to learn about the family of Hazan Dosar.

Application Jacket for Daughter Leathia Ann

Although the original card with wife Sarah and stepchildren revealed that Hazan lived in Mikasukey, Indian Territory, Hazen Dosar died in 1911 in Wewoka, and a small document pertaining to his estate was found establishing his wife and children as heirs. By this time the widow is noted to be Viola, the mother of daughter Dollie.

Details about Hazen's life are scant. Presumably he lived a simple life within the Seminole Nation. His daughters Dollie and Leathia Ann will be the ones through whom his legacy will be continued, and will live through his descendants. We hope the memory of this quiet simple man will not be forgotten.

Heirs to the Estate of Hazen Doser.

BIRTH AFFIDAVIT.

DEPARTMENT OF THE INTERIOR,
COMMISSION TO THE FIVE CIVILIZED TRIBES.

IN RE APPLICATION FOR ENROLLMENT, as a citizen of the _____ Seminole _____ Nation,

of _Leathia Ann Doser_ born on the 5 day of June 1904

Name of Father: _Hagen Doser_ 2026 a citizen of the _Seminole_ Nation.

Name of Mother: _Lucy Sancho_ 2654 a citizen of the _Seminole_ Nation.

Postoffice _Wewoka_

AFFIDAVIT OF MOTHER.

UNITED STATES OF AMERICA, INDIAN TERRITORY,
Western DISTRICT.

I, _Lucy Sancho_, on oath state that I am 21

years of age and a citizen by _adoption_, of the _Seminole_ Nation;

that I am the _not_ lawful wife of _Hagen Doser_, who is a citizen, by

adoption of the _Seminole_ Nation; that a _Female_ child was

born to me on _5_ day of June 1904, that said child has been named

Leathia Ann Doser, and was living March 4, 1905.

Lucy X Sancho
mark

WITNESSES TO MARK:
(Must be Two) Witnesses:
Chas E Webster
Frank L Sabourin

Subscribed and sworn to before me this _10_ day of _May_ 1905

Chas E Webster
Notary Public.

AFFIDAVIT OF ATTENDING PHYSICIAN OR MID-WIFE.

UNITED STATES OF AMERICA, INDIAN TERRITORY,
Western DISTRICT.

I, _Maria Grayson_, a _midwife_, on oath state that I

attended on Mrs. _Lucy Sancho_, wife of

on the _5_ day of June 1904, that there was born to her on said date _Female_

child; that said child was living March 4, 1905, and is said to have been named _Leathia Ann Doser_

Maria X Grayson
mark

WITNESSES TO MARK:
(Must be Two) Witnesses:
Chas E Webster
Frank L Sabourin

Subscribed and sworn to before me this _10_ day of _May_ 1905

Chas E Webster
Notary Public.

Application for Enrollment of Leathia Ann Doser.

Caesar Bruner, Seminole Band Leader

Caesar Bruner
Photo courtesy of Susie Moore, Oklahoma City, Oklahoma.

One cannot present a profile of Seminole families without mention of the name, Caesar Bruner. He was the leader of the Bruner band—the band chief, in fact. And, in addition, his legacy is one that continues to this day. Bruner is also one of the few leaders from Indian Territory for whom there is also a photo image that survives.

At the time of the Dawes Commission, Caesar was already an old man who had arrived with the contingent of Seminoles from Florida. He, like Abraham and others, lived among the maroons and with the Indians who later arrived in the Territory after the Seminole wars. And Bruner, like another compatriot, Dosar Barkus, ended up being not only a band leader, but also a trusted witness who spoke on behalf of many Freedmen who appeared in front of the Dawes Commission in the 1890s and early 1900s. His word was accepted when he spoke on their behalf.

Little is written, however, about Bruner's own family history. In particular, it is seldom mentioned if his own parents and siblings are known. As a result, this is simply a brief overview of his life.

From The Dawes Card

Caesar Bruner lived his life before the Civil War as a free man. He was the son of parents from Alabama and Florida, who came to the Territory during the years of removal. Having been born and having lived among Seminoles as well as Creeks, Bruner spoke the language of both the native people as well as English.

His parents at one time were said to have been enslaved, although that can be disputed to a great degree as well. However, the status given to him on the Dawes Card is interesting. This man, a leader in the tribe, a free man, never enslaved, was still recorded on the Rolls as a "Freedman." His name was recorded on Seminole Freedman card, #740, Field #133. On his card, in fact in the column reflecting the name of the slaveholder, it is clearly written that he was a free man.

Front of Seminole Enrollment Card #133, Field #740.

His parents were said to have been William Bruner and Affie Bruner. According to the information on the Dawes card, they had once been enslaved by Tom Bruner a Seminole.

Siblings of Caesar Bruner

Many of the interviews for Seminoles are missing and not available for examination. Thanks to an interview with one of Caesar Bruner's nephews, a bit more is learned about the family. From the 1937 Indian Pioneer Papers interview with Benjamin F. Bruner, we learned the names of some of Caesar Bruner's siblings. Ben F. Bruner was interviewed as part of the Indian Pioneer project. He spoke in full detail about his life, and his own family.[44]

Like his Uncle Caesar, Ben Bruner was also born free and was part of the same clan of Black Seminoles. And at the time of the Dawes enrollment in the late 1890s, he lived in the same community as his uncle Caesar.

---

[44] University of Oklahoma, Western History Collection, *Indian Pioneer Papers*, Volume 12.

Front of Seminole Enrollment Card #828, Field #221.

Back of Seminole Enrollment Card #828, Field #221.

In the interview for the Pioneer project, he spoke of his own father John and when they came to Indian Territory. His interview also reflects a more intimate relationship between Seminoles enslaved and free, and of the contact between those who were enslaved and those who were identified as full Seminoles. In addition, the relationship between Seminoles and Creeks is also noted in this excerpt from his interview.

And in that interview he mentions his father John's siblings by name. The three siblings were Perry, Caesar, and Will. The surprise was that Perry Bruner (also known as Paro) was a sibling to Caesar. Both of these men were later well-known among Seminole and Creek Freedmen!

3002

BRUNER, BEN F.   INTERVIEW   #12836

Investigator,
Nettie Cain,
January 24, 1938.

                    Interview with Ben F. Bruner,
                    Route 5, Holdenville, Oklahoma.

I was born August 2, 1852, on the banks of the
South Canadian River near Fort Holmes and the old
Government bridge.

My father, John Bruner, was a Creek Freedman who
came from Alabama and my mother, Grace Bruner, was a
full blood Seminole who came from Florida with the
Seminole Indians.

Father was a slave and was sold to Jim Factor for
$3,000.00 in Confederate money. Mother and we children
were not slaves but Father's master allowed him to take
his family when he was sold.

During the Civil War we went to the Chickasaw Nation
and his master would let him rent land and would give him
part of what he made.

Father and one other brother, with their families,
went South during the Civil War, while three other brothers,
Perry, Ceasar and Will, went North with the Seminole Indians
and served with the Union Army until the close of the War.

From this excerpt, we learn that Ben's father, John, had siblings who were Perry, Caesar, and Will. Clearly Caesar is among them. It also has to be pointed out that the brother "Perry" he mentions is actually Paro Bruner, often called Perry even by some by Bruner descendants today.

But note—Paro Bruner was actually enrolled as a Creek, and he was the very first Creek Freedmen to enroll on Census Card #1. Also he is another Freedman leader for whom a rare photo image actually exists as well. When examining the card for Paro Bruner—it is clear that he and Caesar Bruner *were* siblings— same father and the same mother. His parents were William Bruner and Affie Bruner—the same two people who were the parents of Caesar Bruner.

Paro Bruner.
Courtesy of Oklahoma Historical Society.

Front of Creek Enrollment Card #1.

Back of Creek Enrollment Card #1.

Another revelation

The interview with Ben Bruner also left another significant clue about Caesar Bruner. He mentioned that Caesar along with Perry and Will left Indian Territory, and went north (meaning into Kansas) during the Civil War. It was therefore important to examine military records to see if Caesar served in the military in the Union Army.

What a surprise that to see that he did not serve in the military as a soldier, but was possibly a civilian worker with the Indian Home Guards. He applied for a Civil War pension as he stated that he worked for the military as an official interpreter.[45] It does not appear however that he actually received the pension. Later after his death, his widow also applied, but a pension was not given to her, since her husband was not approved to receive one.

---

[45] National Archives and Records Administration. *U.S., Civil War Pension Index: General Index to Pension Files, 1861-1934.* [database on-line]. Provo, UT, USA: Ancestry.com Operations Inc, 2000.

Civil War Pension Index Card for Caesar Bruner.

A second card reflects the brother William, who was a soldier. He enlisted in the 1st Kansas Colored Infantry. That unit was later re-designated as the 79th U.S. Colored Infantry. In his own case, he applied for a pension and received it.

Civil War Pension Index Card for William Bruner.

Application Jacket

Usually the Dawes Commission records contain an application jacket that corresponds with the enrollment card. However, similar to that of the Creeks many of the Seminole files are empty. The jackets exist, but they are clearly marked *empty* and unfortunately in the case of this band leader, his file was also empty. Although he was interviewed many times when other Freedmen members of his band applied, his file was still an empty one years later.

Strangely, in a series of files, the interviews are missing from the file. It is difficult to imagine how the words of a tribal leader would be lost, but some of his words were preserved in another interview when he appeared to select his land allotment.

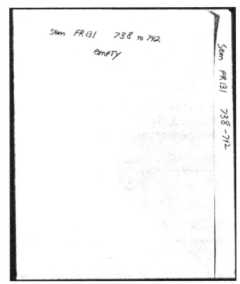

Empty Folder no.742.

DEPARTMENT OF THE INTERIOR
COMMISSION TO THE FIVE CIVILIZED TRIBES
SEMINOLE ALLOTMENT OFFICE
WEWOKA I. T. September 25th 1901

IN THE MATTER OF THE APPLICATION OF Caesar Bruner to take an allotment of land in the Seminole Nation for himself, wife, Nancy Bruner and Grand Daughter, Effie Bruner accompanied by a proper description of the land applied for, the names of said parties being found upon the Seminole Roll approved by the Secretary of the Interior, April 2nd 1901 at Numbers 2337, 2338, and 2339 respectively.

Caesar Bruner being duly sworn testified as follows:

BY THE COMMISSION:

Q. What is your name? A. Caesar Bruner
Q. What is you post-office address. Earlsboro, O. T.
Q. Are a citizen of the Seminole Nation? A. Yes, sir.
Q. What band do you belong to? A. I am Band Chief.
Q. Are you married? A. Yes, sir.
Q. Is your wife a citizen of the Seminole Nation? A. Yes, sir.
Q. What Band does she belong to? A. Caesar Bruner.
Q. Have you ever before this time made application to this Commission for the

persons named in this application to file on any land either in the Seminole Nation, or in any other Indian nation? A. No, sir.

Q. Have you ever before this time made application to this Commission to be enrolled as citizens of any other Indian Nation? A. No, sir.

Q. Are all of the persons named in this application still now living? A. Yes, sir.

Q. Do they live with you? A. Yes, sir.

Q, Do you own a home in the Seminole Nation? A. Yes, sir.

Q, For whom are you selecting a home place? A. My wife.

Q, Are you and the persons whom you represent in actual possession? A. Yes, sir.

Q, You make application for yourself for the E ½ of SE ¼ of the SE ¼ ; the SE ¼ of the NE ¼ of the SE ¼ ; the NE ¼ of the NW ¼ and the W ½ of the NW ¼ of the NE ¼ of Sec 19 of T 10, R 6 containing 90 acres is that correct? A. Yes sir.

Q, Are there any improvements on this land? A. Yes, sir.

Q, Is there a house on it? A. Yes, sir.

Q, Who lives in this house? A. Renters, Adam Stephens.

Q, Does he live there under contract with you? A. Yes, sir.

Q, How many acres under cultivation? A. Forty acres.

Q, Is the improved land fenced? A. Yes, sir.

Q, Does anyone else claim this land or any part of it? No, sir.

Q. Has anyone else any improvements on this land? A. No, sir.

Q. Have you been over this land and examined it with a view of making application for it? A. Yes, sir.

Q. Is it prairie land or timber land? A. It is timber land.

Q. You also make application for your wife, Nancy Bruner for the SW ¼ of SW ¼ and the S ½ of the NW ¼ of SW ¼ of Sec 20, T20, R 6, containing 60 acres is that correct? A. Yes, sir.

Q. Are there any improvements on this land? A. Yes, sir.

Q. Is there a house on it? A. Yes, sir.

Q. Who lives in this house? A. Myself and wife.

Q. How many acres under cultivation? A. Thirty acres.

Q. Is the improved land fenced? A. Yes, sir.

Q. Does anyone else claim this land or any part of it? A. No, sir.

Q. Has anyone else any improvements on this land? A. No, sir.

Q. Have you been over this land and examined it with a view of making application for it? A. Yes, sir.

Q. Is it prairie land or timber land? A. It is timber land.

Q. You also make application for your granddaughter Effie for the SE ¼ of the SW ¼ and the E 20 acres of Lot 4 of Sec 18, T 10, R 6 containing 60 acres, is that correct? A. Yes, sir.

Q. Are there any improvements on this land? A. Yes, sir.

Q. Is there a house on it? A. No sir.

Q. How many acres under cultivation? A. Ten acres.

Q. Is the improved land fenced? A. Yes, sir.

Q. Does anyone else claim this land or any part of it? A. No, sir.

Q. Has anyone else any improvements on this land? A. No, sir.

Q. Have you been over this land and examined it with a view of making application for it? A. Yes, sir.

Q. Is it prairie land or timber land? A. It is prairie and timber.

Q. Will you accept these lands for yourself, you wife, and Granddaughter, as final allotments in the Seminole Nation? A. Yes, sir.

Witness:

W. J. Hastain

Caesar (his X mark) Bruner

Joel ? [illegible]

Subscribed and sworn to me, this 25th day of September, 1901, Wewoka, Indian Territory.

Fred Harry

NOTARY PUBLIC

The result of this interview was that each member of his immediate family was able to select their small multiple acre parcels of land. On this particular document one can see Caesar's name along with wife Nancy, and granddaughter Effie on this land record. It should also be pointed out that Bruner had other adult children as well who received their own land allotments. However, it does appear that in some other cases from other bands that Seminoles identified as By Blood their acreage was even larger, however, how extensive that pattern was is not known. But clearly, the large Bruner clan did occupy much land after the process ended.

It is well known that the large extended family of Bruners settled in the lands around Turkey Creek. An older settlement area known as Brunertown was the area where the Bruner clan of Seminoles lived for many years. After the allotment process ended they lived around Turkey Creek. Caesar Bruner died in 1923 and is buried at Mt. Zion Cemetery in Seminole County, Oklahoma. His descendants now live around the country.

The legacy of Caesar Bruner is an interesting one, going back to his own family in the Seminole Nation, in Florida, and also part of Alabama. By following the footprints that he left in the records, we recognize that his journey was massive. His parents and siblings all survived the Seminole wars, and began a new life with family in Indian Territory. He was a leader to his community and a major patriarch to his family and clan.

Caesar Bruner Application for Homestead Allotment

As one who spoke the Muscogee language of the area, and with him having served the Union army as an interpreter, Caesar Bruner was able to move comfortably among both Seminole and Creek communities. His brother Paro Bruner was a leader among Creek Freedmen while Caesar himself became band chief of the Bruner band. The band still bears his name to this day. His life spanned a good portion of the nineteenth century during a period of disenfranchisement within the other tribes of Freedmen, and he was resilient, through days of hardship after the war, and he prevailed. His life extended into the early years of the twentieth century. He lived to see the world change, to make a difference, and because of him an amazing legacy remains.

Grave marker of Caesar Bruner.
Courtesy of Charles Gibson.

Dosar Barkus, Seminole Band Leader

Though little is known of his early life, Dosar Barkus emerged as one of the leaders in the Black Seminole community of Indian Territory in the late 1890s. Living in the town of Sasakwa at the time, Dosar Barkus appeared in front of the Dawes Commission. The purpose was to enroll himself, his wife Sookie, his sons Daniel and Sango, and daughters Amy and Dolly, and his youngest son Jackson, as Freedmen. At one time he had been enslaved by Seminole leader John Jumper.

Front of Seminole Enrollment Card #660, Field Card #53, for the Dosar Barkus Family.

His father was Joseph Barkus and his mother was Nancy Barkus, and both had been enslaved by John Jumper as well. Sookie's father was Nicholas Patterson, and her mother was Katie Payne. All had been members of the same band.

Back of Seminole Enrollment Card #660, Field Card #53, for the Dosar Barkus Family.

Katie Payne was still alive at the time of the Dawes Commission, and she also had an enrollment card. Her name is recorded on Seminole Enrollment Card #55, along with the name of her granddaughter Bessie Dosar. Katie was at that time seventy years old and was originally from Florida. Like many other Seminoles, she had come to the Territory after the Seminole wars. Katie Payne had also been enslaved by John Jumper. Many of the Barkus band who had been enslaved and who lived in Sasakwa were at one time enslaved by Jumper. Katie identified her father as "Dick," but sadly, as was the case with many who were once enslaved, the name of her mother was unknown. Bessie Dosar was the child of Dosar Barkus and another woman known simply as "Tena," who was by that time deceased. Both Katie and Bessie lived in Sasakawa.

Front of Seminole Enrollment Field Card #55, for Katie Payne.

Back of Seminole Enrollment Field Card #55, for Katie Payne.

Dosar Barkus's Mother Nancy

Upon closer inspection, it appears that Dosar's mother, Nancy, was also still living. She was among some of the oldest Seminole Freedmen at that time. Nancy Barkus also lived in Sasakwa. She had been enslaved by Seminole Mos-ca-diet-chee. Her father and mother were Dick and Tena. Her adult daughter, Mary, the daughter of both Nancy and Joseph Barkus, lived with her. With Mary having the same parents as Dosar, clearly they were siblings.

During the Dawes Commission era, Dosar Barkus became a spokesperson for many of the African Seminoles going through the Dawes admissions process after taking leadership of the Noble Freedman band. By the time of the Dawes hearings he was fifty years old and had a strong constituency in the Seminole nation. This constituency would later depend upon him to get them through the Dawes Commission hearings.

Dosar Barkus witnessed more than fifty interviews for the Dawes Commission, and he was part of their final interview process, vouching for the character and reliability of the data provided to the Commission. It is clear by this respect accorded him at the hearings that his word was to be listened to and followed.

Both Barkus and the other African Seminole band leader, Caesar Bruner, became leaders with very strong levels of influence with a lasting legacy. These two African bands in the Seminole nation still carry the names of Barkus and Bruner after one hundred years. Dosar Barkus went through the land allotment process without difficulty, and none of his claims was contested by anyone regarding his land. Thankfully, the single interview with Dosar Barkus is found with the allotment jackets.

The Dosar Barkus band remains active to this day. The band even has a presence on social media, which offers brief descriptions of their history, beginning with William Noble who led the band from 1870 to 1898. The Barkus band continues to this day.

Front of Seminole Enrollment Card #804, Field Card #197, for Nancy Barkus.

Back of Seminole Enrollment Card #804, Field Card #197, for Nancy Barkus.

The Seminole Freedmen in recent years have had their challenges. They have had to take legal actions to ensure their continued status in the nation. Although the African Seminoles have made some progress, they still struggle for equal treatment by the nation that is their birthright. Clearly, through men like Caesar Bruner and Dosar Barkus the legacy of the Seminole Maroons lives through members of both bands. Their history is one to study, honor, and celebrate. The Barkus descendants are numerous. The history of their band leader will forever be a part of Seminole history.

The Family of Doran and Mary Ann Bruner

From the town of Sasakwa, the family of Doran and Mary Bruner appeared in front of the Dawes Commission to enroll as Seminoles. As written on the enrollment card, Doran was born a free man in the Territory. Yet, as was done with so many, he was placed on the Freedmen Roll. Their children were Alice, Ellen Iona, Eva, Georgeann, Geo. Washington, Manda, and Lizzie. Another child was born in 1905 named Parah Bruner, whose enrollment card is the third image below. This entire family was part of the Caesar Bruner band of Seminoles.

Front of Seminole Enrollment Card #640, Field Card #33, for Doran Bruner Family.

Doran Bruner's father was Dan Bruner, and his mother was Rachel Bruner. Like so many from the Sasakwa settlement, his parents had at one time been enslaved by Seminole John Jumper. Mary Ann's father was Ginford Thompson, and her mother's name was Minerva. Both of her parents were once enslaved by Judge Thompson.

Back of Seminole Enrollment Card #640, Field Card #33, for Doran Bruner Family.

Doran Bruner also had a son Parah, whose name was placed on Seminole New Born Freedman card #7. Both parents' names appear on the card. The "New Born" category appears in most of the tribes, but in many cases some names were simply added on the front of the original family enrollment cards, and in other cases they were placed on New Born Cards such as this case.

Front of Seminole New Born Enrollment Card #7, for Parah Bruner.

Thankfully, a short interview exists for this family. There was most likely additional data in the family's basic file, but the data from that file did not survive. Clearly, questions about the history and parentage of the father and mother would have been taken at the time, but in this case the only document to remain in the file concerns proving the death of one of the children.

Like many of the Seminole Freedmen, a spokesman was called to testify on their behalf. In this case, the band chief, Caesar Bruner, himself came to testify to verify that one of the children had died. Caesar confirmed that Georgeann had died, and that he was at the family home after the funeral. Ben Bruner, an officer for the Bruner band of Seminoles, also came to testify for the family.[46]

DEPARTMENT OF THE INTERIOR
COMMISSION TO THE FIVE CIVILIZED TRIBES
WEWOKA, I. T., August 16, 1900

Seminole Freedman Card.
Field No. 33.

Caesar Bruner being first duly sworn, testified as follows:

Q. What is your name? A. Caesar Bruner.
Q. Are you the band-chief of the Caesar Bruner band of the Seminole Nation? A. Yes, sir.
Q. Do you know Doran Bruner? A. Yes, sir.
Q. And Mary Ann Bruner? A. Yes sir, I did.
Q. Did you know Georgeann Bruner? A. Yes, sir.
Q. Is she living? A. She is dead.
Q. When did she die? A. Last fall, I do not mind exactly what month.
Q. In the year 1899? A. Yes, sir.
Q. Are you certain that it was before Christmas of last year? A. Yes, sir.
Q. Did you attend the funeral? A. I got there, afterwards.
Q. The same day of the funeral? A. Yes, sir.
Q. And the child was already buried when you got there? A. Yes, sir.

Testimony of Ben Bruner

Ben Bruner, being first duly sworn, testified as follows:

Q. What is your name? A. Ben Bruner.
Q. Are you an officer of the Caesar Bruner band of the Seminole Nation? A. Yes, sir.
Q. Do you know the child, Georgeann Bruner? A. No sir, I never seen her.
Q. Did you ever hear of the child? A. Yes, sir.
Q. Whose child was she? A. Doran and Mary Ann Bruner's.
Q. Do you know whether or not this child is living? A. I heard it is dead.
Q. When did you first hear of its being dead? A. As well as I can remember it

---

[46] *Seminole Freedman #33.* Application for Enrollment NARA Publication M1301. (Also accessed from Fold3.com, Native American Collection)

was sometime last October 1899.

* * *

Kate DeBord, being first duly affirmed, states: that as stenographer to the Commission to the Five Civilized Tribes, she reported the above case, and that the foregoing, is a full true and correct transcript of her stenographic notes, taken in said case.

     Kate DeBord

Subscribed and affirmed to before me, this 4th day of September, 1900.

     Tams Bixby

     Acting Chairman

Fortunately there were no complications in the enrollment of this Bruner family. They were allowed to enroll without any challenges made by the Dawes commissioners. Their enrollment however, was that of Seminole Freedmen *"although the father was born a free man, thus never having had to have been 'freed'"* from bondage. Nevertheless, having been approved for enrollment, they were eligible for the allotment of land they which they accepted.

Land Allotment Records

The names of the family are shown on this first image as they applied for their land allotment.[47]

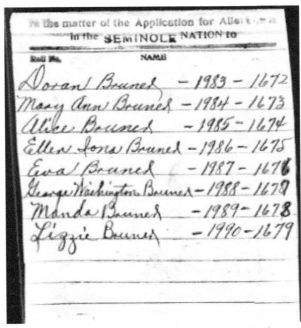

Item from the Doran Bruner Allotment Jacket.

47 Ancestry.com. *Oklahoma and Indian Territory, Land Allotment Jackets for Five Civilized Tribes, 1884-1934*[database on-line]. Provo, UT, USA: Ancestry.com Operations, Inc, 2014.

Much of the data found in the allotment records contain legal descriptions of the land and a focus on improvements if any were made on the land. Most importantly the end of this story is summed up in the final question asked, "Will you accept these lands for yourself, your wife and children as final allotments to the Seminole Nation?" His response was clear, "Yes, sir."

The result of the entire process ended up with each member of this Bruner family receiving their allotment of land consisting of 120 acres for each person.

Document from Doran Bruner Application for Allotment.

Like the story of many Freedmen families, the Doran Bruner family was now a land-owning family, and they were able to face their future moving ahead. Oklahoma statehood came in 1908, and like all families they now faced a new future in the new state of Oklahoma, and a new country—the United States—to call their own. Their legacy however, as Seminoles, like those of the rest of the Five Tribes, was one well documented through complicated years of war, peace, and challenge. This Bruner family, with a legacy originating in Florida, and taking them to Indian Territory, like others of their band, and like others of the same nation, have a richly documented history, reflecting legacy, endurance and continuity. May they always tell their story.

Epilogue

This second volume of *Freedmen of the Frontier* brings to an end my effort to document part of a population that was once forgotten. The story of slavery that occurred upon Oklahoma's soil before statehood is not widely taught, and as a result, the lives of these enslaved are completely overlooked and unknown. I began this project as an effort to put names and faces upon the enslaved and to present a small portion of their family history. My ultimate goal was to put the people back on the historical landscape where they belonged. Freedmen of these five tribes are the sons and daughters of those who helped to create Oklahoma, and through their labor and their resilience, Oklahoma was born.

This project began in 2017, with an idea to simply document one family per week for an entire year. The effort was completed successfully, and I spent most of the following year going through each family story and putting it all into a readable manuscript. Once done, I had over 500 pages of text, which was far too large for a single volume. I then made the decision to make two volumes out of the project. Volume 1, which was published in 2019, includes selected families of Cherokee, Choctaw, and Chickasaw Freedmen families. Volume 2 includes Freedmen families from Creek and Seminole Freedmen families.

My preparation for undertaking this project stemmed from over twenty-five years of researching Freedmen from the territory that became Oklahoma. I came into this work after finding evidence of my grandfather and great-grandparents among a community of Choctaw Freedmen in the Skullyville area. After finding their file, I noticed that I recognized the surnames of others in the same area, and that I had made a discovery. The records I found represented a large community of once-enslaved people whose stories had never been told.

This was "new" history for me. The historical narrative of Oklahoma always includes the Trail of Tears—the end of the journey for the Five Civilized Tribes. But the tears omitted in the story, are the tears of another people also on the same journey, on the same trail and at the same time. Those were the tears of hundreds of African-descended people, purchased in the American South, and taken westward on the same trail, but the travelers were enslaved, and never again would see their loved ones from whom they were taken.

Once in Indian Territory, they were the ones who cleared the land, nursed the children of slaveholders, and who cooked for their families. These enslaved men, women, and children also lost loved ones on the same journey, and some of them died on the trail. But no one wiped their tears. They suffered silently, came to a new land as human property, and yet, through the years, they survived. The challenge for me as a descendant was enormous. I faced a place where slavery in Indian Territory is not taught widely in Oklahoma history, in spite of the fact that the lives of these Freedmen are actually quite well-documented.

A few critical Oklahoma scholars mentioned the Freedmen as footnotes in passing. But thankfully in the 1970s, Arkansas-based scholar Dr. Daniel F. Littlefield became more than curious about the Freedmen, and decided to undertake the effort to study some aspects of "Freedmen" history, placing them on the landscape where they lived, toiled, and died. His scholarship, and in recent years the scholarship of younger researchers, has begun to enlighten this missing chapter of Oklahoma history.

Freedmen of the Frontier is a small attempt to put stories of a long forgotten people in front of the eyes of the larger community of researchers and scholars. May the stories of the Freedmen always be told. May they never be forgotten.

Bibliography

Bateman, Rebecca B. "Africans and Indians: A Comparative Study of the Black Carib and Black Seminole." *Ethnohistory* 1990 (37:1), p.1-24.

Bearss, Edwin. "The Civil War Comes to Indian Territory, 1861: The Flight of Opothleyyoholo." *Journal of the West* 1972 (11:1), p.9-42.

Boyett, Cheryl Race, *The Seminole-Black alliance during the Second Seminole War, 1835-1842*. M.A. California State University, Dominguez Hills, 1996.

Debo, Angie. *The Road to Disappearance*. Norman: University of Oklahoma Press, 1979.

Halliburton, Janet. "Black Slavery in the Creek Nation." *Chronicles of Oklahoma* 1978 (56:3), p.298-314.

Johnson, Charles, Jr. "Black Seminole: Their History and Their Quest for Land." *Journal of the Afro-American Historical and Genealogical Society* 1980 (1:2), p.47-58.

Klos, George E. "Black Seminoles in Territorial Florida." *Southern Historian* 1989 (10), p.26-42.

Krauthamer, Barbara. *Black Slaves, Indian Masters: Slavery, Emancipation and Citizenship in the Native American South*. Chapel Hill: University of North Carolina Press, 2015.

Littlefield, Daniel F. *Africans and Creeks. From the Colonial Period to the Civil War*. Westport: Greenwood Press, 1979.

Littlefield, Daniel F. *Africans and Seminoles. From Removal to Emancipation*. Westport: Greenwood Press, 1977.

Littlefield, Daniel F., Jr. and Underhill, Lonnie E. "The Crazy Snake Uprising"of 1909: A Red, Black, or White Affair?" *Arizona and the West* 1978 (20:4), p.307-324.

May, Katja. *African Americans and the Native Americans in the Creek and Cherokee Nations, 1830s to 1920s: Collision and Collusion*. New York: Garland, 1996.

Mulroy, Kevin. *Freedom on the Border: the Seminole Maroons in Florida, the Indian Territory, Coahuila, and Texas*. Lubbock, TX: Texas Tech University Press, 1993.

Porter, Kenneth Wiggins; Amos, Alcione M.; and Senter, Thomas P. *The Black Seminoles: History of a Freedom-Seeking People 1905-1981*. Gainesville: University Press of Florida, 1996.

Saunt, Claudio. *Black, White and Indian*. Oxford: Oxford University Press, 2006.

Saunt, Claudio. "The English Has Now A Mind to Make Slaves of Them All; Creeks, Seminoles and the Problem of Slavery." *American Indian Quarterly* 1998 (22:1-2), p.157-180.

Searcy, Martha Condray. "The Introduction of African Slavery into the Creek Indian Nation." *Georgia Historical Quarterly* 1982 (66:1), p.21-32.

Walton-Raji, Angela Y. *Black Indian Genealogy Research: African American Ancestors Among the Five Civilized Tribes, An Expanded Edition.* Westminster, MD: Heritage Press, 2007.

Wright, J. Leitch, Jr. *Creeks and Seminoles: The Destruction and Regeneration of the Muscogulge People Indians of the Southeast.* Lincoln: University of Nebraska Press, 1986.

Zellar, Gary. "Occupying the Middle Ground: African Creeks in the First Indian Home Guard, 1862-1865." *Chronicles of Oklahoma* 1998 (76:1) p.48-71.

Index of Names and Places

Made in the USA
Las Vegas, NV
15 September 2022

55333489R00103